PENNSYLVANIA ODDITIES

VOLUME 4

MARLIN BRESSI

Mechanicsburg, PA USA

Published by Sunbury Press, Inc.
Mechanicsburg, Pennsylvania

www.sunburypress.com

Copyright © 2025 by Marlin Bressi.
Cover Copyright © 2025 by Sunbury Press, Inc.

Sunbury Press supports copyright. Copyright fuels creativity, encourages diverse voices, promotes free speech, and creates a vibrant culture. Thank you for buying an authorized edition of this book and for complying with copyright laws. Except for the quotation of short passages for the purpose of criticism and review, no part of this publication may be reproduced, scanned, or distributed in any form without permission. You are supporting writers and allowing Sunbury Press to continue to publish books for every reader. For information contact Sunbury Press, Inc., Subsidiary Rights Dept., PO Box 548, Boiling Springs, PA 17007 USA or legal@sunburypress.com.

For information about special discounts for bulk purchases, please contact Sunbury Press Orders Dept. at (855) 338-8359 or orders@sunburypress.com.

To request one of our authors for speaking engagements or book signings, please contact Sunbury Press Publicity Dept. at publicity@sunburypress.com.

FIRST SUNBURY PRESS EDITION: May 2025

Set in Adobe Garamond | Interior design by Crystal Devine | Cover design by Lawrence Knorr | Edited by Lawrence Knorr.

Publisher's Cataloging-in-Publication Data
Names: Bress, Marlin, author.
Title: Pennsylvania oddities volume 4 / Marlin Bressi.
Description: First trade paperback edition. | Mechanicsburg, PA : Sunbury Press, 2025.
Summary: Strange but true stories of unsolved mysteries, gruesome murders, haunted places and spectacular crimes from Pennsylvania's past.
Identifiers: ISBN : 979-8-88819-308-2 (softcover).
Subjects: HISTORY / United States / 19th Century | HISTORY / United States / State & Local / Middle Atlantic (DC, DE, MD, NJ, NY, PA).

Designed in the USA
0 1 1 2 3 5 8 13 21 34 55

For the Love of Books!

Also by Marlin Bressi:

*Hairy Men in Caves:
True Stories of America's Most Colorful Hermits*

Pennsylvanie Oddities Volume 1

Pennsylvania Oddities Volume 2

Pennsylvania Oddities Volume 3

CONTENTS

CHAPTERS

1. **The Haunted House of Wetmore (McKean County)**..........1
   Wetmore once boasted a mansion with a mysterious past. Rumored to the inhabited by maleficent spirits, the "Haunted House of Wetmore," as it was known to folks in Kane and surrounding towns, was erected in the early 20th century by a businessman who had something of a fire problem—that is to say, every building he owned was destroyed by a bizarre series of fires over several decades for which there was no discernible cause.

2. **The Kensington Killer (Philadelphia County)**..............6
   In June of 1889, a woman was executed at Moyamensing Prison for fatally poisoning her family. This is the chilling story of Sarah Jane Whiteling, an unrepentant killer who holds the distinction of being the last woman hanged in Philadelphia.

3. **The Strange Case of Jeremiah Miller (Cumberland County)**.................................15
   At the turn of the 20th century, the southern slope of Blue Mountain was dotted with log cabins occupied by impoverished folks who eked out a living by chopping wood. One such person was Jeremiah Miller, who, in the summer of 1890, took his own life after slaying his wife. But what makes the tragic tale truly bizarre is that Miller's father and grandfather both suffered similar fates.

4. **Horrors of the Hillside Home (Lackawanna County)**.......20
   The Clarks Summit State Hospital can trace its history back to 1862 when it was known as the Hillside Home. As with any asylum with such a long history, the Hillside Home has seen some dark moments, and the residual energy of those who lived and died at the Hillside Home is said to remain strong to this day, according to those who have worked there.

5. **The Beaver County Axe Murders of 1939 (Beaver County)** .. 29
   In May of 1939, neighbors of the Cook family discovered a bloody axe lying on the ground. Being a farming community, blades and bloody implements weren't terribly uncommon in South Beaver Township, but something about the axe was truly alarming—there was hair stuck to the blade, and the hair appeared to be human.

6. **The Ghosts of Gudgeonville (Erie County)** 34
   Perhaps the most famous haunted location in Erie County is the site of the old Gudgeonville Covered Bridge, which spanned Elk Creek for over a century near a gorge known as the Devil's Backbone. With rumors of paranormal activity stretching back to the mid-20th century, it is no surprise that Gudgeonville has become a favorite spot for ghost hunters. But when it comes to this spectacularly spooky site, what is fact, and what is fiction?

7. **The Tumbling Run Hex (Schuylkill County)**. 39
   In 1911, a bizarre story of witchcraft from Schuylkill County made newspaper headlines across the commonwealth.

8. **Tower City Fugitive: The Hunt for George Wessner (Schuylkill County)** 44
   In March of 1929, the borough of Tower City became the scene of an intensive manhunt. On the loose was 22-year-old George Wessner, an out-of-work miner who fled into the wilderness after murdering his older brother, never to be seen again.

9. **The Strange Confession of Leopold Rowe (Lebanon County)** 49
   From his jail cell in Lebanon, a seemingly harmless vagrant confessed to killing a fellow tramp because he had been tormented, day and night, but the ghostly vision of his victim's face.

10. **Grandpa on the Gallows (Lebanon County)** 54
    In 1887, Annville became the scene of horror after William Showers—the oldest person ever to be executed in Pennsylvania—committed two of the most sensational murders in the history of Lebanon County.

11. **The Murder of Agnes Cooper Wright (Dauphin County)** 61
    The tragic tale of one of the most shocking murders in the history of Dauphin County and how it turned a cold-blooded killer into an overnight celebrity.

12. **The Unsinkable Corpse of Jonas Snyder (Carbon County)** . . . 74
    The bizarre story of one Civil War soldier whose burial at sea didn't go quite as planned.

13. **Cyriacus Spangenberg: The Murderous Minister (Somerset County)** 78
    The historical record shows that 1,043 criminals are known to have been executed in Pennsylvania. Of these, only one was a clergyman—Cyriacus Spangenberg.

14. **Dark Secrets of the Ephrata Cloister (Lancaster County)** 82
    The historic Ephrata Cloister and its museum are visited by hundreds of tourists each year, but some of the sadder secrets of the strange religious sect that once lived here are kept under wraps.

15. **Portrait of an Executioner (Centre County)** 92
    The story of the rise and fall of Frank Lee Wilson is a remarkable tale; it is the tragic story of a quiet, tiny man tasked with the awesome responsibility of meting out justice to the state's most hardened and repugnant criminals. It is a cautionary tale about how a mild-mannered individual can turn into a cruel, hardened shell of a human being in just a few short years after being granted the God-like power of revoking human life.

16. **The Black Phantom of the Scotia Barrens (Centre County)** 101
    Most ghost towns are devoid of paranormal activity, but the ghost town of Scotia is said to be haunted by "Black Bert," who, in real life, was responsible for a brutal slaying in 1910.

17. **The Tragic History of Deadman Corners (Forest County)** . . 109
    Amid the sprawling wilderness of the Allegheny National Forest, miles from the nearest town, four roads converge in a remote spot in Howe Township, where a wooden cross marks the lonesome grave of a murder victim long forgotten.

18. **The Veiled Lady of Penn Park (York County)** 112
   In 1903, the residents of the city of York were terrorized by the nightly appearance of a woman in a long black veil who strolled through Penn Park, imploring frightened passersby to lift her veil and take a peek. As if this occurrence wasn't terrifying enough, it just so happens that Penn Park was once the site of a potter's field where York's impoverished and unknown dead had been buried in unmarked graves, as well as the site of a Civil War hospital.

19. **Buried Alive: The Horrible Death of Mary Newlin (Chester County)** 117
   Sometimes, the killer turns out to be the leader of the search party looking for the victim.

20. **The Disappearing Skeleton (Columbia County)** 125
   In 1926, Royal Phillips ventured into the Brush Valley woods on the grounds of the Roaring Creek Water Company when he stumbled across a human skeleton. Royal picked up the skull and raced back to Mount Carmel to report the ghastly find to the chief of police, and so began a mystery that remained unsolved for nearly a century.

21. **The Ghost Train of Carrolltown (Cambria County)** 128
   In 1892, the citizens of Carrolltown were excited over the coming of the railroad, but the excitement turned to alarm when a phantom locomotive emerged from an unfinished tunnel—an ominous warning of things to come.

22. **The Poisoner of Gray's Alley (Allegheny County)** 133
   One of America's most successful serial killers was Martha Grinder, who rose to notoriety in the years following the Civil War as "The Poisoner of Gray's Alley." What made Martha Grinder so successful in playing her deadly game, aside from the fact that she killed indiscriminately for years before getting caught, was that she appeared beyond reproach—for Martha was regarded as one of the most kind-hearted women in the Pittsburgh area.

About the Author. 139

1.
THE HAUNTED HOUSE OF WETMORE
(MCKEAN COUNTY)

The McKean County township of Wetmore once boasted an architectural gem of a mansion with a dark and mysterious past. Rumored to the inhabited by maleficent spirits, the "Haunted House of Wetmore," as it was known to folks in Kane and surrounding towns, was erected in the early 20th century by a businessman who had something of a fire problem—that is to say, every building he owned was destroyed by a bizarre series of fires over several decades for which there was no discernible cause. Stranger still, several family members of the man for whom the mansion was built died prematurely, leading many to believe that the family of Thomas Keelor had been cursed by someone—or something.

Thomas Keelor, a wealthy lumber merchant, was born in Cincinnati in 1832 and spent his early adulthood in Indiana (the state, not the Pennsylvania county). At the age of 30, he arrived in Pennsylvania with his young bride, Sarah, and made a small fortune in the oil business in Venango County. He invested his earnings by purchasing large tracts of timber around Wetmore and building sawmills, which he connected with his own private railroad. As luck would have it, when oil and natural gas were discovered on one of his properties in 1881, it only added to his wealth, and he soon became one of the most prosperous citizens of northwestern Pennsylvania. Keelor also owned several other businesses in the area, including a chemical plant and a general store. In 1904, he erected a palatial home along Wetmore Road and resided there until he died in 1912 at the age of 80. He also owned a large estate on Fourth Avenue in Warren, which was occupied by one of his sons, Thomas Tod Keelor.

Keelor's death was not a surprise; he had been in poor health for several years, and his obituary warranted a mere three paragraphs in the local paper. The Keelor Mansion continued to be occupied by his widow, Sarah Ward Keelor, until her death three years later (also at the age of 80). As was the custom at the time, both funerals were held inside the home.

While Mr. and Mrs. Thomas Keelor were long-lived, the same could not be said for their offspring. At the time of Sarah's death in 1915, only three of her nine children were still living (so much for genetics), yet none of the children wanted to live in the Keelor Mansion, so it became abandoned. The reason for this is unclear, but it would appear that paranormal activity may have played a role. According to reports, strange sounds were often heard coming from inside the deserted home. The October 25, 1929, edition of the Kane *Republican* states: *It was not long until weird tales of slamming doors and clanking chains and ghostly lights emanated from Wetmore, and the Keelor homestead soon became known as the "Haunted House of Wetmore."*

Although one of Thomas Keelor's sons, Charles, lived just down the road, the home remained uninhabited until 1929, when Rev. Bruce Simpson Wright, an affluent Methodist pastor from Buffalo, purchased it.

As for the three children who were living at the time of Sarah Keelor's demise, these included Thomas Tod Keelor of Warren, Charles Edgar Keelor of Wetmore, and Rebecca Keelor Russell of Warren. Rebecca passed away one year after her mother died in 1916. Thomas Tod died in October of 1917 at the age of 55 after a lingering illness, just two years after his mother. Thirteen months later, Thomas Tod's 22-year-old daughter, Berenice, died suddenly after a brief illness. Thomas Tod Keelor's son, Don Piatt Keelor, passed away in 1943, one week after suffering a heart attack in Kansas City. He was just 55 years of age. Later that year, Charles E. Keelor, who followed his father into the lumber trade, died after a lengthy illness.

Sadly, Thomas Tod Keelor's other daughter, Marjorie, passed away in Warren in 1948 at the age of 56 after a lingering illness, thereby extinguishing the bloodline and bringing an end to a once-prosperous family.

FOLLOWED BY FIRE

Even before the Keelor Mansion burned to the ground, fire seemed to follow in Keelor's footsteps. Keelor's Wetmore sawmill burned down in 1888, while the Keelor Chemical Works suffered a major fire in 1904. Tragically, the chemical plant exploded in June of 1908, killing one worker. The plant reopened and continued to operate until October 3, 1917, when another devastating fire burned the plant to the ground and caused $85,000 worth of damage. The plant in Wetmore manufactured ingredients used for military explosives during WW1, and after the fire, it was believed that "alien enemies," ostensibly German spies, were to blame, though this allegation has never been proven.

Oddly, it seems that October was a curse for the Keelor family; the chemical plant burned down on October 3, 1917. Thomas Tod Keelor died on October 15, 1917. Charles Edgar Keelor died on October 4, 1943. And the Keelor Mansion burned down in October of 1929.

The mysterious fire at the Keelor Mansion occurred at three o'clock on the morning of October 25, 1929, one month after Rev. Wright and his wife had purchased the dormant property. Charles Keelor, who refused to live in the mansion but resided nearby, was the one who first noticed the flames.

According to Charles Keelor, when he reached the mansion, he found that it was engulfed by flames and realized at once that there was no hope of saving it. When he notified the Kane Fire Department, Chief John Valentour said that a five-mile run to Wetmore would be useless, considering the severity of the blaze and the fact that there were no hydrants in Wetmore. As there was no risk of the fire spreading to other dwellings, it was decided to let the fire burn itself out. The Keelor Mansion continued to burn until six o'clock in the morning, and ruins smoldered into the afternoon. By evening, all that remained were the chimneys and cellar walls.

Reverend Wright and his wife, who were at their primary residence in Buffalo at the time, had been making extensive renovations on the old mansion and had hired a contractor, Carl Byham, to replace the roof of the 18-room estate. Byham, whose men had lost several hundred dollars worth of tools in the inferno, was at a loss to explain the blaze; he swore that none of the appliances had been turned on that day and scoffed at the idea that one of his workmen had left a smoldering cigarette inside the building. None of them were at the mansion at the time the fire started.

But what made this particular fire perplexing was the fact that the Keelor Mansion had already caught on fire twice that year. This led many to believe that some less-than-holy types around town hadn't taken too kindly to a preacher moving into the place and had set the fire intentionally. However, authorities refused to believe this theory. As for Rev. Wright and his wife, they were determined to rebuild, even though it was reported that it would take $20,000 (roughly $350,000 in today's currency) to make the structure habitable.

THE BIRTH OF WRIGHTWOOD

Nonetheless, by July of the following year, the Keelor Mansion had been rebuilt by the reverend, who christened his new "summer home" Wrightwood. This, of course, begs the question: "Where the heck did a Methodist minister get the money to buy a lumber millionaire's eighteen-room mansion as a second home?" Upon Wright's sudden death from a heart attack in 1942, his obituary stated that he went directly into the ministry after he graduated from Allegheny College in 1905 at the age of 19, so apparently, preaching must've been a pretty lucrative profession back in the days of the Great Depression. In an ironic twist, Wright's death occurred on the same day as the Cocoanut Grove nightclub fire in Boston, which claimed 492 lives.

The Wrightwood Estate, built upon the foundations of the ill-fated Keelor Mansion, remained the home of the reverend's widow, Margarette, until the early 1960s.

THE LAST KEELOR BUILDING DESTROYED

In the 1940s, an old landmark along Wetmore Road was purchased by local businessman Lloyd Rose and given new life as a drinking establishment. The Colonial Inn, as this business was anachronistically named, was situated on the immense 500-acre parcel of land once owned by Thomas Keelor. The Keelor Mansion had stood not far from this spot, as did the Keelor Chemical Works, and the inn was an immense three-story, fifteen-room structure that Thomas Keelor had originally erected as a general store and office building. After the deaths of his parents, Charles Keelor turned the building into his private residence, and it was from this spot Charles had observed his childhood home being swallowed by flames in October of 1929.

After Charles died in 1943, Lloyd Rose purchased the last remaining Keelor building and turned it into the Colonial Inn, which he ran until he died in 1955. The vacant inn was purchased by J. Algot Swanson and used for storage until May 4, 1958, when a fire of "undetermined origin" sent sparks more than one hundred feet in the air and made the skies glow red for miles, attracting thousands of awestruck McKean County residents to the scene.

The blaze was first discovered at around 10:25 pm by neighbors, who telephoned an alarm to the Kane Fire Department. By the time Fire Chief H.D. Garner reached the inferno, the entire rear of the building was engulfed in fire, and flames had broken through the roof. Although the firemen fought valiantly, no part of the structure survived, and while State Police Fire Marshal John Paxton conducted a full investigation, the cause of the fire could not be determined.

And so ends the strange tale of Thomas Keelor, the cursed man who erected three buildings in Wetmore which all burned to the ground, years apart, under mysterious circumstances. Was it just a matter of bad luck? Was some lifelong enemy of the Keelors lurking in the shadows, waiting to set ablaze everything he had built? Or was some darker force at play?

2.
THE KENSINGTON KILLER
(PHILADELPHIA COUNTY)

June 25, 1889, was a remarkable day in the annals of Pennsylvania crime. On this date, infamous Luzerne County outlaw "Red Nose Mike" was hanged in Wilkes-Barre. Meanwhile, a hundred miles away in Philadelphia, George McCann, who was awaiting trial for crushing his wife's skull with a hatchet, hanged himself inside his cell at Moyamensing Prison. Just a few feet from McCann's cell was the cell of Philadelphia housewife Sarah Jane Whiteling, who was also hanged that very same day. This is the shocking story of the last woman hanged in Pennsylvania—a woman who came to be known as the "The Philadelphia Fiend" and the "Kensington Killer."

In the late 19th century, the neighborhood of Kensington was a soot-stained industrial center dotted with factories and textile mills. Life wasn't easy for the impoverished residents of Kensington; from finding food to put on the dinner table to finding clean air to breath and safe water to drink, every day was a struggle. Among the thousands of working-class poor was John Whiteling, a 38-year-old former streetcar conductor and cigar factory worker who had little trouble finding work but, because of his failing health, had a difficult time staying employed. Because of John's health problems, the Whitelings had bounced around from cheap tenement housing to even cheaper tenement housing, finally settling with his wife and two children on Cadwallader Street in Norris Square.

Sarah Jane Bard was a short, stout middle-aged woman when she married John Whiteling in March of 1880. The daughter of a German immigrant widow, Sarah had arrived in the United States as a nine-month-old child, but her mother passed away shortly thereafter, leaving Sarah in the hands of a family from Iowa. Sarah and her first husband, Tom Brown, moved to Chicago and then to Philadelphia, where Tom was arrested for robbery and sentenced to a long term at the Eastern Penitentiary. He died there, leaving Sara a widow. She became pregnant by the owner of an oyster restaurant and gave birth to a daughter named Bertha. Bertha, or 'Birdie,' as she was called by her family, was just nine months of age when Sarah married John Whiteling. In 1886, Sarah bore John a son named Willie.

Dr. George Smith was the Whiteling family physician and he attended the Whitelings even as the family bounced from apartment to apartment, and it was Dr. Smith who attended to John Whiteling when he fell ill in March of 1888. On March 20, 1888, after days of sickness, John doubled over in agony. While waiting for the arrival of Dr. Smith, Sarah sought the assistance of a neighbor, Mrs. Gilbert, who instructed her to put hot dinner plates on her husband's stomach to relieve his suffering. This seemed to work, but then John began vomiting violently. He died before the doctor could arrive, but Dr. Smith diagnosed his cause of death as inflammation of the bowels.

Being a poor man, John's life was only insured for $145, and his membership in the Benevolent Order of Buffaloes provided his wife an additional death benefit of $85. This money was promptly collected by Sarah Whiteling, who paid $60 in cash for her husband's funeral and used five dollars of the remaining money to buy herself a new watch. Being that John had always been a sickly man and that he carried such a small amount of insurance, very little attention was paid to the matter. But then, just one month later, nine-year-old Bertha Whiteling suddenly fell ill and died. Dr. Smith performed an examination and certified that the child died of gastric fever on April 24, 1888.

When two-year-old Willie was stricken with a sudden illness in May, Dr. Smith was again notified but, sensing that something was not quite right, refused to attend to the sick boy. Another physician visited the Whiteling home on Cadwallader Street, but it was too late. The physician certified the child's death on May 26 was caused by congestion of the bowels. Like John and Bertha, Willie was buried at Mechanic's Cemetery at 22nd Street and Susquehanna Avenue.

THE BODIES EXHUMED

Upon hearing about Willie's death, Dr. Smith notified Coroner Ashbridge. The coroner ordered the bodies exhumed on Wednesday, June 6, but, by some mistake, the exhumation was carried out one day early. When Sarah Whiteling visited the cemetery on Wednesday, she was shocked to find that the graves of her husband and children had been disturbed, and their coffins laid on the grass. She approached the cemetery superintendent and was in the middle of a heated argument when the coroner arrived, accompanied by Dr. Formad, Dr. Stewart and Detective Frank Guyer. The coroner asked Sarah to identify the bodies, which she did, and he and Detective Guyer escorted Sarah to the funeral chapel while the physicians went about their business collecting tissue samples for chemical analysis.

Sarah Whiteling was by no means a bright woman, but she knew what was going on. She grew nervous and began to offer wild explanations as to why the physicians might find a little bit of poison in the bodies of her husband and children. The children had eaten a great deal of candy before they had fallen ill, she claimed, and the owner of the candy shop must've poisoned them. Then she pointed out that the water in her neighborhood was bad, and that must've been the reason why they died in agony. The fact that Sarah herself was still alive and well did little to convince Coroner Ashbridge and Detective Guyer.

A HOUSE FULL OF VERMIN

Professor Leffman analyzed stomach samples taken from the corpses and reported that he had found lethal amounts of arsenic. Sarah was taken into custody and locked up in a cell at the Central Station. The coroner charged her with the murders of her husband and children and told her to call for him whenever she was ready to confess. On June 12, she was ready to confess—at least to two of the murders.

"Our house was full of vermin," she said to Coroner Ashbridge. "In February I bought a box of insect powder with a bellows and used it around the house, but it did no good, so I bought a box of Rough-on-Rats at George Bille's drugstore . . . I asked the clerk what it was, and he said poison and that I should be very careful.

"Some days after this, my husband, having been sick for three or four weeks and not having been out of the house, was very despondent. My husband called me and said he had taken some of that poison I bought. He pointed to a glass on the windowsill that had some sediment in it. He did not say how much he had taken. He took the poison about nine o'clock on Saturday morning, March 17." Sarah then explained how she had appealed to her neighbor for help while waiting for the doctor. He arrived at 1:15 that afternoon. "I did not tell the doctor my husband had taken poison. My only reason for not doing so was on account of the insurance policy declaring that no money would be paid in a death from suicide. My husband never told me why he took the poison, but I think he did it because of our poverty."

Sarah Jane Whiteling insisted that her husband had taken his own life and said that she had made up her mind to do the same. But she couldn't think of what she would do with the children. This was an unusual statement; after all, Sarah had been an orphan herself, and there was no shortage of orphanages around Philadelphia. She then told the coroner that she returned to the drugstore for a second box of Rough-on-Rats a week before Bertha's death.

BEDTIME FOR BIRDIE AND WILLIE

"I gave Bertha the poison. I opened the box and, with a spoon, took out a small quantity and mixed it with water. I called her and said, 'Here, Birdie, is some medicine. I want you to take it nice.' I gave her a teaspoonful every half hour." After a few days, she called for Dr. Smith, who left medicine powder. Sarah admitted that she did not give the medicine to Bertha until shortly before her death. "I only gave her the poisoned water every half hour," she admitted. "I felt sorry for having given her the poison and stopped giving it, and then I gave her the medicine for the first time." Bertha died on the morning of April 24. Sarah told the coroner that

Bertha's life was insured in the John Hancock Company for $122, which she later received.

After Bertha's death, Sarah rented out the bottom floor of her home to Mrs. Donovan while she moved into a third-story room with two-year-old Willie. On Thursday morning, May 24, she began feeding the rat poison to Willie and then once again sent for Dr. Smith, who gave her more medicine powder. "I did not give Willie any of the medicine which should have been given every half hour," Sarah confessed. "The next morning, I received a letter from Dr. Smith saying I should get another doctor, as he did not wish to attend Willie after having lost my husband and Bertha," she continued.

"Mrs. Gilbert recommended Dr. Dietrich. He came, and I showed him Dr. Smith's letter. He read it and then prescribed powders every two hours. I gave him three of these before he died. I stopped giving him the poison on Friday morning and then wanted to save him, but it was too late to do so." Sarah admitted that she had insured the child's life one week after the death of her husband. "I received $17 from Prudential and $30 from the Hancock Company," she said. "I did not poison all of them at one time for fear I would be found out, so I thought I would poison them one month apart, then no one would suspect me," she added.

As for her motive, which was clearly financial, Sarah told the coroner that she was actually doing her children a favor by murdering them. "My only notion for poisoning my children was that Birdie might grow up to be sinful and wicked, as she had at various times stolen pennies from people and once a pocketbook from her teacher at the school at Hancock and Thompson streets," said Sarah. "She was very sinful for one so young, and I did not want her to grow up and become a great sinner."

When it came to Willie, on the other hand, Sarah's motive was purely selfish. "My little boy was sinless, and I poisoned him because he was in the way," said Sarah. "He was a burden to me. Without him, I could get along. Now I know my children are angels in heaven, and I want to meet them there when I die. I do not expect to meet my husband there because he committed suicide, and a suicide cannot go to heaven." This statement speaks volumes about the depths of Sarah's depravity and delusion; though she admitted to killing her own children, she seemed confident that she would face no repercussions in the afterlife for her earthly deeds. In her warped mind, Sarah was nothing less than a hero for rescuing her children from their very own existence.

NEIGHBORS CALL FOR HANGING

After Sarah Whiteling's confession, indignation ran high throughout Kensington, but when it was discovered that Sarah, in order to divert suspicion, had also given poisoned candy to the young son of her next-door neighbor, scores of men and women alike said they hoped to see her hang. "She's a villain," declared Sarah's next-door neighbor, Mrs. Martin. "One of my little boys is sick in the country now since he ate candy that was given to him by Mrs. Whiteling. My boy was taken sick at the same time as her Birdie, and when her child died, Mrs. Whiteling told a neighbor she was surprised that my child was still living." She also said that her husband caught Sarah giving the candy to their children and that she didn't seem the least bit saddened when Bertha drew her last tortured breath.

But what Mrs. Martin said next was beyond chilling. "She told me that she had eight children," said the neighbor, "but didn't say what had ever become of them."

Mrs. Martin also made statements that seemed to prove that the murders had been premeditated. Sarah had sold Willie's clothing and rocking chair to a neighbor for a quarter while the child was still in the early stages of poisoning, and a few days before John Whiteling fell ill, Sarah took him and the children to a portrait studio to have their photographs taken—something the family had never done before. It was as if Sarah knew they would be going away very soon and wanted something to remember them by.

THE DOCTOR'S STATEMENT

"Now that Mrs. Whiteling has confessed, I would say that the diseases all resembled arsenical poisoning, but no physician would suspect that it was arsenical poisoning unless his attention was directed that way," explained Dr. Smith to the *Philadelphia Times*. "I had attended the family for years. Whiteling was a man prone to sickness and prone to complain while sick. I had attended him for a rheumatic ailment shortly before his last illness. Mrs. Whiteling seemed to love her children very much at times . . . then I would notice an indifference which I could not understand."

Dr. Smith had been treating another girl with gastritis at the time he was treating Bertha, and he was inclined to believe that Bertha was suffering from the same ailment since the two cases were so similar. "I had up to Bertha's death not the slightest suspicion that the deaths were not perfectly legitimate," he said. As for Willie's illness, Sarah told him that he had collided with another boy while running down the alley and began suffering stomach pains shortly thereafter. Of course, even if this statement were true, it certainly wouldn't have secured Mrs. Whiteling a nomination for Mother of the Year, as it's rarely a wise idea to allow your two-year-old to run loose in the back alleys of Philadelphia's dirtiest and roughest neighborhoods.

"I told Mrs. Whiteling that I would not attend the boy," explained Dr. Smith, "and gave as a reason that, there having been already two deaths in the family, I would not be doing justice to her or myself if I did attend him." He then told her that she would have to find another doctor.

"When I saw the announcement of Willie's death, I immediately went to the coroner and told him of the deaths, which I then thought suspicious, and told him that although they might be perfectly legitimate, they were worth investigating."

CONFESSION AT THE INQUEST

Up until June 15, the day of the inquest, Sarah insisted that her husband's death had been a suicide. But after being taken from Moyamensing Prison to the coroner's office, she admitted to Coroner Ashbridge and Detective Guyer that she had poisoned her husband by slipping arsenic into his egg nog.

"We were very poor," she sobbed after confessing to her husband's murder. "So poor that we owed everybody—the grocer and everybody else. The insurance money I got on my husband only did for a little while. And then I thought about what was placed on Bertha's life." At this point, Sarah buried her face in her hands and refused to say another word. The coroner's jury, after a brief deliberation, declared that Bertha, Willie, and John Whiteling came to their deaths from arsenic poisoning at the hands of Sarah Jane Whiteling. She was taken back to Moyamensing Prison to await trial.

THE POISONER'S DOOM

On the evening of Wednesday, November 28, 1888, a jury—for only the second time in the long history of Philadelphia—found a woman guilty of murder in the first degree. But it was not the quick and easy verdict many had predicted; when the jury went out, they stood eleven to one, and it took two hours for the others to convince the lone holdout that the death penalty was appropriate for Sarah Whiteling's premeditated and selfish actions. When the verdict was finally read, Sarah's eyes were red from weeping, but otherwise, she did not react.

On December 22, Sarah was brought to court for sentencing before Judge Allison, who had already overruled the motion for a retrial put forth by defense attorneys George Arundel and Henry Paxson. Despite the packed court room, Sarah appeared composed and serene while her attorneys fidgeted anxiously. "If the prisoner had been convicted of a petty crime, she could not have appeared more indifferent to her fate," reported the *Philadelphia Times*. The judge regarded Sarah with a stern yet pitying gaze as he asked if she had anything to say before the sentence was passed. The defendant smiled and whispered to her lawyer. "She has nothing to say," he told Judge Allison. The judge then spoke in a voice quivering with emotion.

"The facts of your crime were not only denied by your counsel but confessed by you. These confessions disclosed a willful, deliberate and premeditated purpose to destroy life, and your motive for doing so was stated without reserve. But beyond this confession, the testimony disclosed the fact that you profited pecuniarily by the death of each of your victims. The only defense which was or could be made for you was that of insanity. After a careful re-examination of the evidence, I am unable to find anything that would have justified a verdict of not guilty on the grounds that you were not a reasonable and accountable person when you destroyed the life of your daughter, Bertha.

"In each instance in which you destroyed life there was a motive assigned for the commission of the crime wholly inconsistent with the existence of an irresistible mania or impulse. Having reached this conclusion, it only remains for me to perform my last solemn duty, which the law imposes on me. The sentence of the court is that you, Sarah Jane Whiteling, be taken hence to the jail of the County of Philadelphia, from whence you came, and that you be there hanged by the neck until you are dead, and may God have mercy upon your soul."

THE EXECUTION

On the morning of Wednesday, June 26, 1889, Sarah ate a breakfast of fried eggs, toast and chocolate before being removed from the female ward and transported to the male ward. In the corridor stood the scaffold on which she would shortly be hanged. She passed her final hours in prayer with her spiritual adviser, Rev. William D. Jones, and undertaker Samuel Kehr. Together, they sang "There is a Fountain Filled With Blood" (religious hymns were apparently quite morbid back then) before Warden Krumbhaar and the prison physician arrived to lead the short, solemn procession to the scaffold.

It was a fearless and smiling Sarah Jane Whiteling who marched to the gallows in the center of the prison corridor, but the bravery was just an act; once she climbed the twelve steps of the scaffold, her legs grew weak, and she trembled like a leaf. "Dear God, hear me!" she cried. "Do not leave me. Savior, have mercy!" Witnesses remarked that they could hear her short, rapid breaths from the far end of the corridor as the hangman dropped to his knees and bound the condemned woman's ankles. Then he stood and slipped the black cap over her face. The noose was placed around her neck.

A guard stationed on the upper rail stood with his hand raised. When the guard's hand dropped at 10:07, the trapdoor of the scaffold flew open, and Sarah Whiteling dropped, her neck breaking instantly. In contrast to the ceaseless days and nights of incomprehensible agony that she had bestowed upon her husband and children, Sarah's death was merciful and quick. After thirty minutes, her body was cut down and turned over to Dr. Alice Bennett of the Norristown Hospital for the Insane, who wished to examine the killer's brain (it was later reported that Sarah's brain was completely normal). Afterward, she was buried at Mechanic's Cemetery in Philadelphia alongside the husband and children she had murdered.

In 1950, the city of Philadelphia relocated Mechanic's Cemetery and the neighboring Odd Fellows Cemetery to construct low-income housing on the thirty-acre site, which had been a burial ground since 1849. Over 60,000 bodies were moved to Lawnview Cemetery in Montgomery County, including the bodies of Sarah Jane Whiteling and her victims.

3.
THE STRANGE CASE OF JEREMIAH MILLER
(CUMBERLAND COUNTY)

At the turn of the 20th century, a new village sprouted across the Susquehanna River from Harrisburg. Spurred by the growth of the Pennsylvania Railroad, this village—which came to be known as Enola—was named for the daughter of a farmer from nearby Summerdale. But long before Enola became the site of the third-largest rail yard in the country (now owned by Norfolk Southern, the Enola Yard currently handles 275,000 tons of freight per day), this region was sparsely populated. The southern slope of Blue Mountain, which divides Cumberland and Perry counties, was dotted with log cabins, primarily occupied by impoverished folks who eked out a living by chopping wood, mending pots and pans, and performing odd jobs around the countryside.

One such person was Jeremiah Miller, who rose to infamy in the summer of 1890 after slaying his wife and taking his own life. But what makes the tragic tale of Jeremiah Miller truly bizarre is that his father and grandfather both suffered similar fates.

In a lonely cabin that once stood where Tower Road now runs lived Jeremiah, his wife, Mary Ann, and their nine children, who ranged in age from two months to 17 years. Three other children had died in infancy.

The Millers were a very poor family; Jeremiah earned money by chopping pine, which his wife and children sold throughout East Pennsboro Township. Mary Ann, despite her rugged disposition, was said to be a pretty woman—and it was this physical trait that filled him with jealousy and led to many vicious quarrels, which often culminated with Jeremiah reaching for his shotgun and threatening to kill his entire family.

On Tuesday morning, July 29, 1890, Mary Ann had gone to Camp Hill to sell wood, and when she returned, she found herself embroiled in yet another heated argument with her jealous husband. The argument was renewed the following morning, with Jeremiah accusing his wife of infidelity. It was Jeremiah's brothers who had filled the woodsman's head with all sorts of ideas, but whether these accusations were true or not, no one will ever know—because Jeremiah, in a fit of rage, picked up a double-barreled shotgun and fired a heavy load of buckshot into Mary Ann's left side at close range as she was nursing their youngest child. Upon realizing what he had done, Jeremiah rushed from the cabin, leaned against the fence, and pointed the muzzle of the shotgun to his belly. With the aid of a stick, he condemned himself to death in a deafening instant, though death was slow in arriving.

The gruesome tragedy was witnessed by all nine of the Miller children, and they ran down the mountain screaming and spreading the alarm. But while the shooting had occurred around nine o'clock in the morning, no one appeared on the scene until noon. It was undertaker Jacob Stauffer of Camp Hill, accompanied by Constable Charles Burns, who reached the cabin first. They were joined a short time later by Dr. Heckert of West Fairview, who was astonished to discover that Mary Ann was still clinging to life, though the wound had left her paralyzed from the waist down. Constable Burns attempted to impanel a jury, but Justice of the Peace M.H. Rupley intervened, declaring that he should hold the inquest, which he scheduled for nine o'clock the following morning.

THE INQUEST

A handful of woodsmen from the mountains and farmers from the valley gathered outside the tiny cabin on Thursday, July 31, awaiting the arrival of Squire Rupley. Meanwhile, the unburied body of Jeremiah Miller sweltered outside the cabin in the hot sun. The jury included Constable Burns, Undertaker Stauffer, H.S. Glessner, John Roth, John Bixler, Solomon Seifert and Harvey Gutshall. It was the mortally-wounded Mary Ann Miller who testified first at the inquest. Despite the gaping wound in her side and complete paralysis of her lower extremities, she was able to provide the following testimony:

"My husband quarreled with me at the breakfast table on account of some lies which had been circulated. He threatened to kill me and, jumping from the table, took down a double-barreled muzzle-loader and walked outside the cabin. Said he would blow us all up with the gun. As I turned from the table, he dropped me from the load of buckshot, which entered my side and arm. Jere then said, 'Now I have killed Mom. Now Pap will blow his own head off.' It was near dinnertime when anyone came up the mountain. Shot me at nine o'clock. I have worked hard . . . could not do enough for him. Worked from morning until night."

Martha Miller, the 17-year-old daughter described by the Carlisle *Sentinel* as a "pretty and modest mountain girl," was the next to testify. "I was at home when the shooting occurred," she said. "Father had been mad at us all on account of some lies some parties had told about us. Accusing us of running around with the boys and said mom was not to be trusted. Just as he shot Mom, I came down the road, and Pop pushed me aside. He stood on a stone in front of the gate when he said he was going to blow his head off and put an end to this berry-picking business." She then described how Jeremiah had used a stick to pull the trigger and shoot himself.

"As soon as he shot, he called for us to come. We all came to him. I went to him. He said he wished he hadn't fought with us. I brought him water, and he drank it. He said we were to put water on him as his clothes were burning. He then died. I saw him shoot mother. His brothers made up a lot of lies and said mother and I were running around with other men. Said time and again he would kill us. On Saturday evening, he came home from West Fairview and said he would kill us. Two weeks ago, he wanted to go and hang himself. He had some notes coming due and did not have the money to meet them. He was troubled about money matters—amount, about fifty dollars."

The jury retired and returned a few minutes later with a verdict that Jeremiah Miller "came to his death by a gun shot wound inflicted by his own hand, caused by financial and family trouble."

As soon as the inquest was over, the stench from the undressed, unwashed corpse necessitated its prompt burial, though opinion was divided over where and how it ought to be disposed. The leading opinion, as expressed by the local farmers, was that it should be thrown into a pit on the mountain, which the locals used for the disposal of deceased horses. It was the dead man's dying victim who finally demanded that her husband be given a proper burial. At her direction, one of the jurors rummaged through the cabin and found a receipt for a burial plot that the deceased had purchased in the Zion Luthern Church cemetery.

Armed with this certificate, Undertaker Stauffer and Squire Rupley transported the putrid remains down the mountain by wagon. No mourners or relatives followed the wagon to the churchyard, and no service was held at the graveside because the reverend refused to participate. The coffin was taken from the wagon and placed under a tree beneath the blazing July sun until the grave was dug, but there was one tiny problem—no one wanted to dig it. Squire Rupley begged and pleaded, but nobody wanted to have anything to do with the tragic affair. The grave was eventually dug by Squire Rupley himself and a reporter from a Carlisle newspaper, as they were the only ones who remained at the graveyard, save for a black dog, attracted by the stench, who kept scratching at the coffin as the two men toiled beneath the searing sun, and a drunkard who offered to recite a graveside sermon in exchange for a barrel of beer. Squire Rupley declined the offer.

DEATH CLAIMS A WIDOW

Dr. Heckert and Dr. Basehore, whose examination revealed that Mrs. Miller had suffered a severed spinal column, both knew that the wounded woman would never recover, though they were unable to predict her demise. "Death may come at any hour," Heckert told reporters, "yet she may linger for weeks." Mary Ann Miller finally passed away on August 3 and was laid to rest alongside her husband. While the local gossip hounds had besmirched Mary Ann's reputation, others insisted after her death that she couldn't have been anything less than a faithful wife. After all, hadn't she, in her dying condition with a feeble voice, saved her monstrous husband from the ignominious fate of a pauper's grave?

Of the nine orphaned Miller children, not much is known, except that one teenage daughter was adopted a short time later by Mr. and Mrs. Francis Fink of Mechanicsburg and another daughter was adopted by Mary "Aunt Polly" Turns of Rockville. One of the Miller children, Mary (born 1872), married Charles Wiseman of Steelton and died at the age of 32 from complications during childbirth. Another daughter, Margaret, was later adopted by Ellsworth McKinley of Harrisburg.

THE KISSEL MURDER

Today, the cemetery adjoining the red-brick Zion Lutheran Church is known as Enola Cemetery. Not far from the graves of Jeremiah and Mary Ann Miller is a weathered tombstone bearing a still-legible inscription: In memory of John Kissel, assassinated on June 29, 1856. A peculiar coincidence in this story is that two men were arrested, tried, and convicted over Kissel's murder. One of them was Abraham Miller—Jeremiah's father.

John Kissel was a farmer from East Pennsboro and was said to be an eccentric bachelor of peculiar habits. His body was discovered in the yard beside his house on June 30. A physician examined Kissel's body and found one gunshot wound in the heart and another in the left eye. There were no witnesses to the crime, but suspicion eventually fell upon a black man named Matthew Willis, who was seen flaunting large sums of cash after Kissel's death. After Willis was arrested, police found $43 in gold coins and $85 in bills in his wallet. Willis admitted that the money had belonged to Kissel, but it had been given to him by Abraham Miller. According to Willis, Miller had murdered the bachelor farmer and had given him the money to hold onto, believing that he would eventually be suspected of killing Kissel.

Miller was soon arrested and lodged in the Carlisle jail. On September 1, 1853, he took his life by tying his handkerchief around a bar in the door of his cell and strangling himself. Willis, who was convicted for his role in the murder, also died in the Cumberland County jail.

Strangely, Abraham Miller's father—Jeremiah's grandfather—also committed suicide on the mountain north of Enola around the same time that Abraham was arrested for the murder of John Kissel. According to newspapers, when his body was found, it had been picked apart by crows and buzzards.

4.
HORRORS OF THE HILLSIDE HOME
(LACKAWANNA COUNTY)

In 1862, the residents of Providence Township in Lackawanna County decided to establish a poor farm for those who were impoverished, handicapped, elderly, and otherwise unable to work and care for themselves. As the population of Lackawanna County grew, the facility, which was then known as the Hillside Home, also provided housing and treatment for the mentally ill. In 1943, the name was changed to the Clarks Summit State Hospital, which continues to operate to this day.

As with any asylum with such a long history, the Hillside Home has seen some dark moments, but none so tragic as the brutal murder of two female inmates in the summer of 1906 by a deranged mute named Ignatz Krewzyk.

Slaughter in the Sewing Room

Ignatz Krewzyk was 28 years old when he was committed to the asylum by Poor Director Frank J. Dickert in 1899 for wandering the city of Scranton in a delirious state. Though he was penniless, unable to speak, and afflicted with deafness and depression, Krewzyk (some reports spell his surname as Krawczyk or Krewzyp) had never exhibited any signs of violence. As the years went on, he earned the trust of staff members and eventually became something of a jack-of-all-trades around the institution, serving at various times as a handyman, barber, mechanic and kitchen helper. Because of his good conduct, Krewzyk was granted a considerable amount of liberty at the Hillside Home and was considered a harmless sort of fellow.

So, then, it was no cause for alarm when Ignatz Krewzyk appeared at the dispensary door at the asylum's infirmary on the afternoon of Wednesday, July 18, 1906. Dr. M.J. Ruddy, an intern under the direction of resident physician Dr. William Lynch, was busy receiving patients and treating their illnesses and injuries. When the intern's back was turned, Krewzyk reached inside his medical bag. Perhaps it was the gleam of the surgical implements that had aroused his curiosity, or perhaps the inmate had been biding his time to carry out a premeditated act, but, for whatever reason, Krewzyk decided to steal a 12-inch amputation knife from the doctor's bag and leave the infirmary without attracting anyone's attention.

It took only a moment for Dr. Ruddy to realize that his knife was missing, however, and the intern followed Krewzyk into a corridor. The inmate, upon realizing that he was being followed, suddenly grew aggressive; brandishing the weapon in his hand, he ran to the administrative office across the hall where the superintendent's daughter, Miss Josephine Beemer, was chatting with Catherine Heckle, the niece of Director A.W. Paine. Catherine and Josephine fled from the office, screaming when the inmate entered the room. They sprinted down the corridor with Ignatz Krewzyk hot on their heels.

The screaming of the young women attracted a keeper named Richard Davis, as well as Lieutenant George Paine, who was Catherine's cousin and a West Point cadet, and Josephine's brother, Floyd Beemer. Paine and Beemer, along with Davis and Dr. Ruddy, were able to corner the madman in one of the offices. With rare courage, Davis slowly approached the knife-wielding inmate and convinced him to take a seat. With an outstretched hand, he calmly made his way to Krewzyk, and the inmate showed signs of cooperation. But then, in an instant, Krewzyk's face flashed with rage. He lunged at Davis, thrusting the weapon into the keeper's torso, penetrating the lung and intestine.

As Davis fell to the floor, the sight of the blood only served to arouse the mute maniac. He raised the knife and was poised to strike his victim again, but Floyd Beemer swung a wooden chair into the back of Krewzyk's skull with such force that it broke the chair's leg—though it did not seem to faze the attacker. Paine and Beemer ran out of the room in search of a heavier weapon, but Krewzyk seized the opportunity to escape. The men raced after the inmate, following him up the stairs to the second floor.

On the second floor of the Hillside Home was the sewing room. It was here where Ignatz Krewzyk encountered two of the female inmates, 53-year-old Annie Golden and 66-year-old Missouria Ann Van Valen. They had probably greeted him with a smile; Krewzyk had spent the morning helping them move things around inside the sewing room and had worked alongside the women in the kitchen of the Hillside Home for several years. Krewzyk plunged the knife into Mrs. Golden's abdomen up to its hilt. He withdrew the blade and stabbed her again before turning his attention to Mrs. Van Valen. Krewzyk drove the bloodied blade clean through her breastbone with ease and withdrew the blade so viciously that it left a gaping wound from her chest to her navel.

The women in the sewing room had already fled in terror, and Krewzyk sought refuge from his pursuers behind a sewing machine. George Paine struck the inmate's arm with a chair, breaking the blade of the knife and stunning the madman. Before Krewzyk could recover, Paine and Beemer threw him to the floor until someone was able to restrain him with a straitjacket. Krewzyk was then taken to a cell, apparently oblivious to the tragedy he had wrought upon the Hillside Home.

Meanwhile, attention was being given to the victims. Mrs. Golden and Mrs. Van Valen had died before falling to the floor, and Keeper Davis was gasping for his life. His chances for survival appeared slim.

Later that evening, Coroner James Stein arrived at the Hillside Home and consulted with Drs. Lynch, Ruddy and Paine over the condition of Richard Davis. They decided against examining the wound; due to the great depth of the gash, probing the wound might cause further damage, and Davis was already in shock. They summoned Dr. S.P. Longstreet, who examined the wound and spent the night taking care of Davis. According to Dr. Longstreet, two deep incisions had been made by the surgical knife.

The first incision, three and a half inches long, penetrated the lung and severed cartilage in the ribcage, loosening three ribs. The second wound, three inches in length, left an opening in the stomach from which Davis' intestines protruded. Coroner Stein stated that an inquest would not be held until Mr. Davis' fate was determined.

Superintendent George Beemer, who had managed the Hillside Home for twenty years, was deeply affected by the tragedy. When reporters asked him about the murders, he was at a loss for words. Richard Davis, however, began to show signs of improvement and answered reporters' questions from his bed. "I was foolish to go near that man with the knife," Davis stated the morning after the attack. "I never saw him in that condition before, and I did not think he would stab me, as I always had perfect control over him."

But, in addition to sadness and confusion, the tragedy at the Hillside Home also produced anger. Because of state law, keepers of insane patients were not allowed to carry weapons in the facility. "The absence of a weapon of defense yesterday made possible the casualties," declared the Scranton *Tribune* on July 19, while the Scranton *Truth* opined: "The lesson that this should teach is that the insane are always dangerous. There is no such person as a harmless lunatic." The Tunkhannock *New Age* went even further, declaring: *It may be set down as a fact that there are no really insane people who are not dangerous. No matter how docile, a sudden impulse to murder may spring upon them . . . Insane persons are universally acknowledged to be irresponsible.*

As for Ignatz Krewzyk's motive, Dr. Lynch believed that his mind had snapped because of overwork. July 19th had been "moving day" at the Hillside Home, and the inmate had been moving heavy furniture and lugging boxes up and down stairs since early morning. It was reported that the killer, a Polish immigrant, had no friends or family in the United States, and he had not received a single visitor during his seven-year stay at the facility. District Attorney W.R. Lewis, meanwhile, stated that he wasn't sure how to proceed with Krewzyk's prosecution; there was no doubt that the man was insane, but a trial would just result in him being sentenced to another insane asylum. Whatever became of the killer is a mystery, though it is evident that Krewzyk never again tasted freedom.

On July 31, after Richard Davis was on his way to making a full recovery, a coroner's jury exonerated the Hillside Home and its staff for any wrongdoing. Four months later, Dr. William Lynch resigned his position as resident physician of Hillside Home, ostensibly to devote more of his time to his private practice. His letter of resignation to the Poor Board did not refer to the murders.

SCANDALS AT THE HILLSIDE HOME

While the murders of Missouria Ann Van Valen and Annie Golden were soon forgotten, Hillside Home would once again be in the headlines for all the wrong reasons in May of 1907 after the death of an elderly inmate named James Edmunds. Relatives of the deceased made shocking allegations of inhumane treatment, which led to an investigation of the facility and its practices. Mary Edmunds, sister of the deceased, told reporters that the Hillside Home had waited several weeks to inform the Edmunds family about James' death—presumably to cover up the fact that an examination by the Edmunds family physician, Dr. C.E. Thompson, revealed that James had suffered a broken jaw sometime earlier, which was left untreated until Edmunds died a slow, agonizing death by starvation. Only then did the Hillside Home telephone his relatives. The coroner refused to definitively state the cause of the man's death, though his report revealed that, in addition to a broken jaw, Edmunds had a deep bruise over his left eye. The Edmunds family claimed that James had been clubbed to death by a nightkeeper named Savage, though the official position of the Hillside Home was that the inmate had died from uric acid poisoning. Telephone calls from concerned newspaper reporters to Superintendent Beemer went unanswered.

On May 29, 1907, the coroner's jury inquiring into the death of James Edmunds returned an appalling verdict, asserting that the deceased came to his death by natural causes. Attorney John R. Jones, representing the Edmunds family, called several witnesses to the stand, only to have their testimony stricken down as irrelevant or inadmissible by Coroner Stein at the objection of the Hillside Home's attorney, Harold Scragg. As a result, the jury was instructed to disregard the testimony of former keeper Thomas Thomas, who had admitted on the witness stand that he had used a club to quell an unruly patient several years earlier—an incident that led to his termination. Perhaps that was the right call, as Thomas had left the facility long before the death of James Edmunds. However, Thomas' testimony would have established a precedent for the cruel and barbaric treatment of inmates.

In February of 1908, Richard Davis—the keeper who Ignatz Krewzyk had stabbed—filed a $100,000 suit against the Scranton Poor District for injuries he suffered at the Hillside Home, alleging that the director and superintendent had been negligent in permitting Krewzyk to roam the facility freely. His lawyer, John R. Jones, also claimed that physicians had left Davis lying on the ground for eleven hours before he received any medical attention.

Two months later, the family of Owen Gallagher asked police to investigate his death after his brother Patrick discovered bruises and cuts on Owen's forehead, nose, lip, and cheeks when the body was shipped home for burial from the Hillside Home. Management, not surprisingly, claimed that Gallagher's death had been completely natural.

More than a decade later, in November of 1919, new startling allegations surfaced that rocked Lackawanna County. This time, an undercover probe by New York investigators hired by the American Red Cross revealed that the management of the Hillside Home had engaged in abuse, graft and other forms of corruption. The two New York detectives—a man pretending to be a dope fiend and a woman hired as a nurse—spent two weeks at Hillside Home. During that time, the male detective lost 22 pounds due to the treatment he received from staff. "I have been in prisons and reformatories in all parts of the United States on detective work," he reported to Ralph Weeks, the chairman of the investigating committee, "but never in all my travels have I encountered such a place as the Hillside Home." His report also found that employees had been stealing large quantities of food from Hillside's storerooms, including 1,700 bushels of potatoes, leaving the inmates with one potato per week. Even though the Poor Board owned a large herd of cattle, the detective did not see an ounce of milk, a pat of butter, or beef during his two-week stay.

These accusations inspired Governor Sproul to launch his own probe. On November 6, Sproul appointed Bromley Wharton as chairman of the investigating committee. The investigation was dropped after just a few weeks. However, in February of 1920, the Central Labor Union adopted a resolution calling for the governor to reopen the investigation, alleging that patient cruelties had been "hushed up" and "whitewashed" by Wharton. Nothing ever came of this effort, and, once again, the alleged perpetrators escaped penalties.

BEATEN TO DEATH BY GUARDS

On September 18, 1923, 40-year-old inmate William Burgerhoff—the burly, athletic son of a prominent Scranton businessman—died at Hillside Home under mysterious circumstances. Superintendent A.T. Rutherford, suspecting foul play, immediately notified District Attorney Harold A. Scragg (who had successfully defended the Hillside Home seventeen years earlier after the death of James Edmunds), and it was concluded that Burgerhoff had been beaten to death by two guards, Harold Duffy and Paul Salai. Duffy, who secured employment by using the alias of "Harold Williams," fled the scene. Both men were eventually indicted on murder charges, though, once again, the Hillside Home was cleared of any wrongdoing.

It was the Scranton *Times* who discovered that the reason why Duffy had sought employment at the Hillside Home under an assumed name was because he had been fired from the Farview State Hospital for the Criminally Insane for serious rules infractions. Nevertheless, management was never held accountable for this deadly oversight. Willard Matthews, president of the Scranton Poor Board, argued that there was no reason to criticize the Hillside management. "The Burgerhoff case is one that might happen at any similar institution," stated Matthews. "There might be a repetition of it next week."

Not surprisingly, when Harold Duffy was tried before Judge Edwards the following November, he was acquitted of all charges by the jury. Because District Attorney Scragg was unable to secure a conviction against Duffy, the charges against Paul Salai were dropped. This outrageous verdict caused one local paper, the Carbondale *Daily News*, to publish the headline: SCRANTON A SAFE PLACE FOR MURDER. In a rare move, Judge Edwards publicly criticized the jury for its verdict, declaring that

Lackawanna County juries were "not measuring up to their responsibilities," adding that they had been "entirely too lenient" with defendants accused of heinous crimes.

Sadly, Burgerhoff wasn't the only patient killed by Hillside Home keepers. In 1932, 61-year-old Lewis Goldberg died just days after he arrived at the institution, and Coroner Bartecchi's autopsy revealed that Goldberg had suffered a ruptured kidney, three broken ribs, bruises on his face and possibly a fractured skull. The ensuing investigation discovered that Goldberg had been severely beaten around 3:30 on the morning of October 6 by two keepers, John McTague and William Tobin, and two inmates who had assisted them by holding Goldberg down. Following the struggle, Goldberg was treated for a bloodied nose by Hillside Home physicians, who somehow managed to overlook his severe internal injuries. He was taken to the hospital and died about fifteen hours later.

Deputy Coroner Mackey stated that the Hillside Home's failure to furnish Goldberg with proper medical attention came "close to being criminal negligence." However, the part of the tragedy that struck Mackey as being the most odd was the fact that Goldberg's underwear had been changed sometime between the time he was assaulted and taken to the hospital. "Someone changed those underclothes," said Mackey. "They were wet, but not with blood." This strange detail was also observed by undertaker Louis Ziman, who stated that it was customary for the Hillside Home to turn over the bodies of deceased patients nude and wrapped in a sheet. "This was the first time I got a body from the home with underclothes on," Ziman remarked.

As was the case in the deaths of James Edmunds, Owen Gallagher, and William Burgerhoff, the Hillside Home failed to notify Goldberg's family until several hours had passed after he had been pronounced dead. This delay allowed Hillside Home staff to cover their tracks and dispose of incriminating evidence (such as Goldberg's underwear), or so some newspaper reporters claimed. McTague and Tobin, along with patients Joseph Murphy and James Shea, were arrested and charged with murder but got off with a slap on the wrist; McTague and Tobin each received 1-2 year sentences from Judge William Leach after the jury recommended "extreme mercy."

In 1938, the Shapiro Act was passed, which directed the state to take over county and municipal mental institutions. This act was the result of Senator Shapiro's effort to stamp out inmate abuse after an investigation of the Dyberry Hospital near Philadelphia revealed acts of "cruelty and barbarity reminiscent of the Dark Ages." According to the scathing Shapiro Legislative Committee report, the Dyberry investigation found 200 male inmates without clothing, several inmates who had been kept in straitjackets for over three years, and noted that the facility's food cart was being used to transport the dead. Tuberculosis and sexually transmitted diseases—passed onto inmates from staffers—ran rampant though the children's ward. When the bill was finally signed into law in May of 1943 after passing through the House by a vote of 115 to 51, the Hillside Home, along with the Blakely Poor Farm and the Ransom Poor Farm, became property of the Commonwealth of Pennsylvania. From that time forward, the institution became known as the Clarks Summit State Hospital.

While state control did succeed in curbing (though not completely stopping) inmate abuse, the residual energy of the men and women who lived and died at the Hillside Home is said to remain strong to this day, according to those who have worked there. Former employees have reported cold spots in hallways and the feeling of being watched, and others have reported hearing the ghostly sounds of muffled weeping coming from an upstairs maintenance closet. One local paranormal researcher who recently explored the Clarks Summit State Hospital Cemetery said that she felt an uncomfortable "strangled feeling" around her neck, which caused her to abandon her investigation.

5.
THE BEAVER COUNTY AXE MURDERS OF 1939
(BEAVER COUNTY)

It was a Wednesday morning in May of 1939 when neighbors of the Cook family made a startling discovery—a bloody axe lying on the ground. Being a farming community not far from the Ohio state line, blades and bloody implements weren't terribly uncommon in South Beaver Township; the necessities of daily life often required the butchering of a chicken or the slaughtering of a pig. But there was indeed something about the bloody axe that was very uncommon and grounds for some concern—there was hair stuck to the blade, and the hair appeared to be human. That the axe was found on the property of Forrest Cook, a township tax collector, seemed to indicate the possibility of foul play. After all, few folks are as unpopular as the local tax collector. The neighbors—Walter Gratz, Edward Younginger, John Knowlson, Robert Davis and Ted Young—got in their car and drove back to Blackhawk to call the police. Sheriff Kennedy and Deputy Sheriff Dindinger left for the Cook homestead at once.

Four miles to the south of the Cook place, Walter Gratz, the operator of the service station on the Old Blackhawk Road, had suspected that something might've been amiss earlier that morning when a black 1939 Buick sedan stopped for gas at around seven o'clock. It was Forrest Cook's car, and Gratz knew Mr. Cook quite well—but the driver was Forrest's teenage son, Paul. When Gratz noticed that Paul was acting strangely, the teenager said that $800 was missing from the Cook home and that his parents and sister had disappeared. The boy believed that they might've gone to the World's Fair in New York, for they had left their son fifty dollars and a note saying that they'd be back in a few days. Gratz, who found the story rather fishy, promptly gathered up some neighbors and drove to the Cook place to investigate but were prevented from entering by the family's dogs, who were barking ferociously in the yard. Within the hour, troopers from the Butler barracks of the State Police would be inside the home, counting the dead.

Just like the concerned neighbors and Sheriff Kennedy and his deputy, Sergeant Frank Milligan and Private Jacob Hanicheck had also been prevented from entering the property by the growling of the two hunting dogs in the back yard. These were Paul's fox hounds, Towser and Old Sam, which had been given to him by his father when the boy was just three years of age. As the lawmen drew closer, they realized that Old Sam wasn't much of a threat, for he was toothless and nearly blind. The troopers entered the home, and it didn't take them long to find the bodies of Forrest, his wife, Cora, and their daughter, Eleanor. They were upstairs, still in their beds in the single room they shared. The killer had slaughtered them while they were sleeping. Their bodies were also riddled with holes, blasted at close range with a shotgun.

The room was a shambles; blood was splattered everywhere. Even the hardened troopers found it difficult to look at the terribly mangled bodies on the beds, as did Coroner H.C. McCarter, who soon arrived on the scene. Neighbors were questioned, and it was learned that Paul had been butting heads with his father for some time. Forrest had recently refused to allow Paul to get his driver's license, and the teenager had been brooding ever since. But even more damning was the fact that Paul's empty bed was right next to that of his 25-year-old sister, Eleanor. Their beds were tucked behind the chimney, which divided their side of the bedroom from that of their parents. How had Paul managed to avoid the killer? Sergeant Milligan of the State Police had no choice but to believe that Paul had been the one who had wielded the axe. He immediately requested the Butler barracks to send out a teletype message, reading: *Wanted for suspicion of murder. Paul J. Cook, 17, looks older, five feet eight inches, 160 pounds, stocky build, dark hair, brown eyes, dark complexion. Driving Buick sedan, color black. 1939 model. No operator's license. Believed owned by the victim, his father.*

WITHOUT THE SLIGHTEST REMORSE

Chained in the barn on the adjoining farm of Robert Groetzinger were Old Sam and Towser, the fox hounds that had belonged to the suspected killer. For days after the murders, Old Sam howled mournfully in the neighbor's barn. Forrest had given him to Paul when Sam was just a puppy, but age had robbed the hound of its teeth and half of its eyesight. Towser, who was just a few years younger than Old Sam, was totally blind.

"I was there that morning eleven years ago when Forrest gave Sam to the kid," recalled Groetzinger when he spoke to a reporter from the *Pittsburgh Post-Gazette*. "How happy the kid was." He stopped to look over toward the Cook farm, now crawling with newspapermen and curiosity seekers. "I was over there this morning, too. Well, they're all gone now. All but Paul, and I guess he won't be coming back. I guess it's up to me to put Old Sam and Towser out of the way."

Just six hours after the police issued the bulletin, Paul Cook was apprehended in front of Beaver Falls High School by Private Hanicheck. The teenager was in his father's car with his friends, talking about their "hot dates" for the evening. He was taken back to the scene of the crime and made to look upon the gruesome carnage he had wrought. "There was just a trace of tears as he stood and looked down at his mother, but that was all," stated Sergeant Milligan. Paul expressed no emotion when he looked at the mutilated body of his father. Paul was taken to the Beaver Falls police station for questioning, and it wasn't long before his icy demeanor melted, and he calmly and nonchalantly confessed to the ghastly crime in front of Assistant District Attorney Ralph E. Smith.

Puffing repeatedly on a cigarette, the teenager said that he left his home Tuesday with three other boys. First, they drove into Ohio to purchase a bottle of gin, then proceeded to Rochester, where they bought another bottle of gin and a pint of whiskey. From Rochester, they drove on to Beaver, stopping to fish in a stream before growing bored and deciding to go for a swim at Montgomery Island Dam. That evening, the friends went to a carnival in Vanport before returning to their homes around midnight. Paul awakened his father accidentally while getting into bed, and Forrest, smelling liquor on the boy's breath, gave him a stern lecture. This was the offense that drove Paul Cook to murder.

Paul stated that he waited until his father had gone back to sleep before slipping outside to the spring house and grabbing an axe. He grabbed a shotgun from downstairs and then went back to bed, hiding the weapons beneath his blanket. It was around a quarter after three in the morning when he crept out of his bed and struck his father with the blunt end of the axe. Then he struck his mother. This caused his 25-year-old sister, Eleanor, to awaken. Paul pointed the shotgun at her and fired into her face at point-blank range. He fired again at his mother, then picked up the axe and mutilated his three victims.

Next, Paul went downstairs, washed up and put on a change of clothes. He returned the gun to its customary place, then went to the spring house and drank a bottle of soda. Armed with his father's keys and the money from his wallet, Paul drove to a diner for an early breakfast, then into Beaver Falls, where he purchased a pair of white shoes. After eating a second breakfast in East Palestine, he decided to stop at the home of Mrs. Lydia Wilson, pretending to be upset over the disappearance of $800 in tax money from the family home. This was the same cover story he would later tell to Walter Gratz at the service station in Blackhawk.

After filling up the Buick with gas, Paul picked up three girls and drove to a garage in Beaver Falls, where he had a mechanic install a new radio, mirrors and other accessories. "Just charge it to my dad," Paul told the mechanic when he was presented with the bill.

The assistant D.A. was shocked by Paul's lack of remorse. "This boy is not insane, for he recited all of the cold-blooded facts without a tremor," said Smith. "There was no emotion is his face or voice. This is one of the most ruthless slayings in the history of Beaver County."

After questioning, Paul was taken to the courthouse, where he repeated his statement to the district attorney and then to the county jail. In the meantime, the bodies were taken away to the funeral parlor of Orville Scott in Beaver Falls. When Paul was asked if he wished to attend the funeral services, he just shrugged and asked for a cigarette. The victims were laid to rest at Highland Cemetery, not far from the Cook home.

On May 26, Paul Cook waived his preliminary hearing and was formally arraigned before the magistrate, George Niver, on three charges of first-degree murder. In June, Judge Frank Reader appointed a lunacy commission to determine Paul's sanity at the request of his aunt, Jeanneau White. If found insane, Paul would be spared life imprisonment at Western Penitentiary.

A KILLER LEARNS HIS FATE

Wearing the white shoes he had purchased on the morning he had slaughtered his parents and sister, with the money he had stolen from the taxpayers of South Beaver Township, 17-year-old Paul Cook stood before Judge Reader and learned his fate. On September 6, the lunacy commission determined that the teenager was legally insane. But Judge Reader issued a stark reminder to the youth, in case he had thought that he'd gotten off easy: Should Paul ever regain his sanity, he would be required to stand trial for murder.

That day finally came in September of 1963. After being an inmate at Farview State Hospital for twenty-four years, Paul Cook, now 41 years of age, was pronounced sane and ordered to stand trial. At the hearing, Assistant District Attorney Joseph S. Walko told the jury that the only fair verdict would be not guilty by reason of insanity, while Dr. John Shovlin, superintendent at Farview, testified that Cook suffered from a persecution complex that had afflicted him since his early teens. According to Dr. Shovlin, Cook had no awareness of what he had done for seven years; he wasn't able to face reality until 1946 and didn't make a full recovery until 1957. Shovlin insisted that Cook no longer presented a danger to himself or others.

After deliberating for ninety-five minutes, the jury rendered a verdict of not guilty. Paul Cook was released from custody and moved to East Palestine, Ohio.

6.
THE GHOSTS OF GUDGEONVILLE
(ERIE COUNTY)

Perhaps the most famous haunted location in Erie County is the site of the old Gudgeonville Covered Bridge, which spanned Elk Creek for over a century near a gorge known as the Devil's Backbone. With rumors of paranormal activity stretching back to the mid-20th century—and a verifiable track record of bizarre deaths—it is no surprise that Gudgeonville has become a favorite spot for ghosthunters. But when it comes to this spectacularly spooky site, what is fact, and what is fiction? Before we explore the legends, let's delve into the history of the bridge and the surrounding area.

Located just south of I-90 in western Erie County in Girard Township, the Gudgeonville Bridge was an 84-foot-long covered bridge erected in 1868 over Elk Creek, which flows into Lake Erie at a point near Erie Bluffs State Park. According to local historians, the bridge foundation was constructed of remnants from the Beaver & Erie Canal (also known as the Erie Extension Canal), which was constructed between 1831 and 1844 and ran for 136 miles from Lake Erie to the Ohio River, bisecting Elk Creek at the village of Girard. If you're curious about how a canal crosses a creek, the answer is an aqueduct, which was erected 96 feet above the water level of the creek (the aqueduct over Elk Creek Gorge collapsed around 1871).

Elk Creek carves a serpentine gorge through most of Girard Township, and the two branches of Elk Creek (Elk Creek and Little Elk Creek) converge at a rock formation known as the Devil's Nose. A short distance to the south is the natural curiosity known as the Devil's Backbone, and it is between these spots where a covered bridge was erected to provide access to Gudgeonville, which wasn't actually much of a town but the site of a 19th-century factory which manufactured gudgeons, a type of fitting used in canal and shipping locks. Historic maps show the location of this factory at a spot on the west side of Beckman Road, near its intersection with Tannery Road. During its heyday in the 1880s, Gudgeonville boasted a handful of homes, stores and even a schoolhouse, which operated into the early 1900s.

History records at least three catastrophic fires that struck the Gudgeonville covered bridge; the first occurred in the 1870s and resulted in the rebuilding of the bridge. Another fire, causing $3000 worth of damage, took place in April of 1965 and was believed to have been set intentionally. The fire that finally destroyed the bridge, which was listed on the U.S. National Register of Historic Places in 1980, occurred on November 8, 2008, and was determined by the State Police to have been a case of arson. The two men, both of whom had extensive criminal records, were arrested, tried and convicted.

THE LEGENDS OF GUDGEONVILLE BRIDGE

The bridge has played a starring role in local legend since the early 1900s. According to several websites, a headless horseman supposedly haunted the bridge during the era, and witnesses claimed that phantom hooves could be heard when the bridge was still standing. Of course, there is no record (at least that I could find) of anyone losing a head in the vicinity.

Another popular legend pertains to the name of Gudgeonville. Supposedly, Gudgeon was the name of a mule who refused to cross the bridge during the mid-19th century and toppled over dead of a heart attack from fright. As the story goes, the mule's owner buried Gudgeon on the west bank of Elk Creek and had the name of his beloved mule painted on the bridge entrance. The name sort of stuck, and locals took to calling the spot Gudgeonville. Of course, this tale couldn't possibly be true since the bridge in question hadn't been constructed yet (although an earlier bridge most likely stood at the same spot).

However, the most often-told ghost tales involve the screams of a young girl who fell to her death from the Gudgeonville cliffs in the 1940s. Surprisingly, there may actually be some truth to this legend. My research turned up three people who actually plunged to their deaths in the vicinity of the bridge, though the earliest of these deaths took place in 1955. Strangely, all of these deaths involved victims between the ages of 10 and 15.

THE DEATH OF RUBY SHORTS

At 2:00 in the morning of Sunday, September 18, 1955, a 15-year-old girl from Union City named Ruby Eleanor Shorts was killed instantly when she and her 46-year-old companion, Ralph Blaser, mysteriously fell from a 180-foot cliff into Elk Creek at Gudgeonville during what newspapers reported as a "moonlight stroll." According to the Kane *Republican*, the girl and Blaser were with a carload of people, including Ruby's mother, when they parked near the bridge, and the two victims went for a walk alone. While Blaser would later recover from his injuries, Ruby's death was ruled accidental by the police, who, for some reason, weren't too curious as to why a 46-year-old man would go for a walk on the edge of a cliff with a 15-year-old girl at two o'clock in the morning.

THE DEATH OF DARLENE NICHOALS

On Monday, April 20, 1964, a 10-year-old girl from Girard named Darlene Nichoals plunged 225 feet to her death from the Gudgeonville cliffs. According to newspaper reports, Darlene and her mother had gone to the cliffs for a picnic, and the young girl fell over the edge while attempting to pick up some moss. The *Latrobe Bulletin* reported that two college students found the girl's body in Elk Creek and that Darlene was pronounced dead on arrival at St. Vincent Hospital.

THE DEATH OF GERARD SERFOZO

Of the handful of verifiable deaths that have occurred near the Gudgeonville Bridge, none is as strange as the 1965 death of a 15-year-old seminary student from Erie named Gerard Serfozo. On Thursday, April 1, 1965,

Gerard and a group of about a hundred students from the Divine Word Catholic Seminary in nearby Girard went hiking in the vicinity of the Devil's Backbone. Gerard told a priest that he was going back and instructed the others in the group to meet him at the Gudgeonville covered bridge. It was the last time anyone would see him alive.

Two days later, after an extensive search by more than 200 volunteers, including the State Police, Civil Defense units and Boy Scouts, Gerard's body was discovered by firemen in a flat-bottom boat shortly before 10:00 a.m. on the banks of Elk Creek, about a quarter mile downstream from the bridge. Deputy Coroner Wallace Mulligan made an identification at the scene, and the death was later ruled accidental by Erie County Coroner Merle Wood. An autopsy revealed that Serfozo had died from drowning after sustaining injuries from a fall.

What makes this death so baffling is that hundreds of people searched for Gerard Serfozo for two days, only to find him a short distance from the bridge where he planned on meeting up with the rest of the group. Though his death had been caused by drowning, his body was found on dry ground. Also interesting is the fact that Serfozo was a Boy Scout and an expert swimmer.

Yet another thing that makes this case so fascinating is that the Gudgeonville covered bridge was intentionally set on fire just two days after the discovery of the body. On Monday, April 5, 1965, the fire caused an estimated $3000 worth of damage to the covered bridge, and although police concluded that arsonists had burned the bridge, no arrests were ever made. Could there be some connection? For now, this will have to remain a mystery. Forty-three years later, arsonists would finally succeed in destroying the historic structure for good—though the destruction of the Gudgeonville bridge didn't put an end to the ghost stories.

THE LEGACY OF THE BRIDGE

After arsonists destroyed the bridge, Girard Township supervisors salvaged what they could, and, for years, the wooden remains were housed in a field. In the summer of 2020, township supervisor Clay Brocious invited residents to take home a little piece of the legendary bridge, and Erie County residents were eager to accept the invitation, much to his surprise. "The final count was, I think, 163," Brocius told *YourErie*. "The response was phenomenal, overwhelming, and it just goes to show how important this bridge was to a lot of people around here."

Of course, it has been reported that spirits can attach themselves to physical objects, so if you're one of the 163 lucky owners of a chunk of the Gudgeonville Covered Bridge and have been noticing some strange sights and sounds around your home, then it just might confirm that the ghost stories may have some truth in them after all.

7.

THE TUMBLING RUN HEX

(SCHUYLKILL COUNTY)

In 1911, witchcraft hysteria spread across central Pennsylvania, with dozens of superstitious citizens swearing out complaints against men and women accused of being hex or "pow-wow" doctors. In February, infamous hex doctor Elmer Palm was arrested in Berks County and charged with "causing the nervous breakdown" of a woman named Mrs. Maddiman after he claimed that he could break every bone in the human body just by casting a spell. In December, the well-known witch of Nuremberg, Lena Fogel (who was no stranger to jail cells herself), was found dead in her hut on the Schuylkill-Luzerne County line with a bottle of laudanum by her side. Between these local newsworthy events, however, was a bizarre story of witchcraft from Schuylkill County, which made newspaper headlines across the commonwealth.

Alleging that her father, 61-year-old Howell Thomas of Tumbling Run, died as the result of a hex placed upon him by a family from Orwigsburg, Mary Isabelle Thomas went to the press with a long list of peculiar incidents which she believed would prove that her father succumbed to the effects of black magic. Mary claimed that the evil spell had the power to prevent Thomas' guns from shooting, thereby leaving him vulnerable and unprotected and that several cows had died under mysterious circumstances. While there might have been a perfectly reasonable explanation for these misfortunes, the item that caught people's attention was the daughter's claim that these mishaps began immediately after a black cat showed up on the Thomas farm—a cat that assumed monstrous proportions, growing to four feet in height before magically returning to its previous form.

After these misfortunes began, the Thomas family called a witch doctor, who claimed that a well-respected Orwigsburg family, the Potts, was conspiring to steal their wealth through supernatural means, warning them to be prepared for a visit from the spell-caster in the near future. Adding a new level of drama to the affair was the fact that one of Howell's daughters, Elizabeth, had married into the Potts family.

Sure enough, the alleged witch from Orwigsburg, Elizabeth Howell Potts, soon came calling—armed with a black cat. It wasn't long before Howell Thomas suffered a massive stroke. Within five months, he would be dead. Howell's death came as a shock to many; he was a man who always enjoyed excellent health. Though he was a veteran of the Civil War, he refused to accept a soldier's pension. Perhaps it was because of this heartiness that Howell's family, especially brother William and daughter Mary Isabelle, refused to believe that he had died of natural causes.

According to William, his niece had also fallen gravely ill around the same time as Howell Thomas. Two prominent physicians examined the girl but held little hope for her recovery. Gradually, she grew weaker until death seemed to be sitting at the foot of her bed. This deathwatch continued for eight weeks until the "spell" suddenly broke. "The Demon has evidently determined to get the remainder of the family," declared William, "and in this, he may succeed."

PANIC AT THE FUNERAL

Howell Thomas, a native of Pottsville, was a former miner who had taken up farming later in life. From his deathbed, he insisted upon having his funeral at his old house in Pottsville, and this final request was carried out by his brother William, who lived at the farm, his wife Lenore, and his daughters, Mary Isabelle and Elizabeth. On the morning of September 26, Howell's remains were taken from the undertaking parlor of T.D. Bergen to the old home at 301 North Third Street. About two dozen guests and relatives attended what was intended to be a simple affair; there were no flowers, and mourners paid their last respects before the open casket, where Howell lay atop a lining of white silk, attired in a black suit and white shirt. But then, all hell broke loose.

It was Mary Isabelle who, just before the service began at three o'clock, refused to allow her sister Elizabeth into the house when she arrived with her husband, Albert, and their three children, claiming that she had been the one responsible for the hex. As soon as Elizabeth entered the house, Mary Isabelle had come running downstairs, ordering her sister out of the building before swooning and falling into a dead faint. Friends eventually resuscitated her with smelling salts, though Elizabeth chose to wait outside while the services continued.

Afterward, they all went to the Odd Fellows Cemetery, where another dramatic scene unfolded. Elizabeth dropped her knees at the side of the casket and wept. "My God, father!" she cried. "I did not know I was accused of anything until I saw it in the papers, and they wouldn't let me see you while you were alive." Mary Isabelle loudly remarked that this was a lie.

KILLING A HEX CAT

After the funeral, those who believed William and Mary Isabelle's claim about the giant hex cat determined to find it and kill it with a golden bullet. Early before sunrise on Wednesday morning, September 27, neighbors descended upon the Thomas farm at Mary Isabelle's request. According to Mary, the witch doctor had instructed her to melt a five-dollar gold coin and make bullets with it, as this was the only way the evil cat could be killed. The neighbors were eager to participate in this strange hunt, as many of them claimed to have seen the giant beast with their own eyes prowling around the farm before sunrise.

The "hex cat," of course, failed to make its customary pre-dawn appearance that day, but the local farmers blamed themselves for this failure. Some had carried Bibles with them and others had brought along crucifixes, and they fervently believed that they had unintentionally frightened the evil spirit away. Mary Isabelle pledged to try again on her own, and her gun, loaded with a golden bullet, never left her side.

On September 30, it was reported that the infamous hex cat had been captured and was in the possession of a Pottsville furniture store manager named Kelliher. When the *Republican* sent a reporter to the store, Kelliher stated that it was one of his salesmen, Charles Lawless, who had heard the wailing of a small child in distress while passing through Tumbling Run. Lawless traced the cries to a hollow tree trunk and found a cat he believed to be the diabolical feline, which he trapped in a box and brought back to the store. The following morning, workers entered the store and found everything a shambles. According to Kelliher, the horses for the wagons refused to eat, and the telephone refused to work. The crate in which the hex cat had been placed was empty, but one of the workers located it on a store room shelf. Fearing a bite from the magical beast, nobody dared to touch it, and one worker was so frightened that he resigned his job on the spot. After catching the cat, Kelliher decided to have it displayed inside his shop and offered a gun loaded with a gold bullet to anyone who dared to shoot it. Witnesses who came to view the animal remarked that it was a "medium size" back cat and weighed around "two or three pounds." While the publicity stunt worked, papers neglected to mention just how many of these curiosity-seekers purchased furniture during their visit.

Sightings of the hex cat continued for months, though the fantastical feline always managed to escape with all nine of its lives intact. In January 1912, it was reported that witchdoctors had devised a novel plan to negate the evil spell of the hex cat by obtaining a magical cat of their own. In nearby Schuylkill Haven, local pow-wow doctors found themselves a "hexahemeron" cat, so named because it had been born on the sixth day of the sixth month of 1906 and was the sixth kitten of the litter. The theory behind this cat's magical powers was that the official Bible contained five books of Moses (the Pentateuch), even though a sixth book was written but never "made the cut." This missing book of Moses features the Witch of Endor, who supposedly bestows cats with the power of warding off evil spirits.

Despite their use of an "anti-hex" hexahemeron cat, strange things continued to happen at the Thomas farm to the bafflement of local witch doctors, and each tragedy—whether caused by nature or caused by witchcraft—was reported by local papers, whose curious readers thirsted for more information. Most journalists, however, scoffed at the idea of a hex; a newspaperman from the Pottsville *Republican* had visited the farm after Howell Thomas' stroke and reported that "conditions may be described as pitiful," that the house was "badly in need of repairs," while the animals and cattle were "half-starved looking." A fine apple orchard situated on the property was untended, and the reporter noted bushels of fruit decaying on the ground for lack of a harvester. When asked why they hadn't sold the fruit to earn money for the necessities of life, the Thomas family claimed that the hex had poisoned the apples.

Register of Wills H.H. Seltzer probated the will of Howell Thomas in March of the following year. It was one of the shortest wills ever probated in Schuylkill County. Containing twenty words and written on a ragged scrap of paper, the document, dated May 17, 1910, declares: *To my brother, William Thomas, and my daughter, Mary Thomas, all that is mine is thine.*

THE AFTERMATH

Had the Thomas family and some of their superstitious neighbors been laboring under a delusion that Elizabeth Potts had cast a magical spell? Or was there some dark family secret that inspired Mary Isabelle to make such spectacular accusations against her sister? It seems that Mary must have believed the delusion wholeheartedly, as she never recovered from the experience. Armed with her golden bullet, she remained unmarried for the remainder of her life, eventually dying in poverty at the county almshouse on May 13, 1944, at the age of 67.

Strangely, Elizabeth Howell Potts—the accused witch—died 25 days later at the age of 64, preceding her husband in death by two years. Ironically, both sisters are buried alongside each other at Salem Evangelical Cemetery in Orwigsburg. It was reported after her death that Elizabeth was the last surviving member of the Thomas family. One of Elizabeth's sons, Howell Franklin Potts, later became a judge of elections, a position he held for fifteen years until his premature death in 1955 at the age of 48. Like his grandfather, his death was caused by a stroke.

8.

TOWER CITY FUGITIVE: THE HUNT FOR GEORGE WESSNER

(SCHUYLKILL COUNTY)

In March of 1929, the Schuylkill County borough of Tower City became the scene of an intensive manhunt. On the loose was 22-year-old George Wessner, an out-of-work miner who fled into the wilderness after murdering his older brother, never to be seen again.

On the evening of Monday, March 18, an argument took place between George and his 32-year-old brother, William, inside the living room of their home on the corner of Sixth and Wiconisco streets. George and William had been at odds for several months, and the brothers often went weeks without speaking to each other. Shortly after 8:00 that evening, William was reading in the living room when George came downstairs and said calmly, "Bill, I'm going to shoot you."

"Quit your kidding," replied William, without looking up from his book. George made hos way to a cupboard and seized a .38 caliber revolver. William threw down his book and raced for the door. He had only made it about fifty feet when five shots rang out. The last bullet struck William under the right arm, penetrating the lung. George fled the scene while his dying brother staggered to the home of a neighbor, Jacob Houtz. "George did it," gasped William, clutching his chest and falling onto a couch in Houtz's kitchen.

Houtz immediately summoned help, and Dr. Stutzman, a local physician, raced to the Houtz home at 507 Wiconisco Avenue, where he found William Wessner conscious, but his efforts to stop the bleeding were futile. William died at 8:48 without revealing a reason for the shooting. Their widowed mother, Mrs. Agnes Wessner, was at church at the time of the shooting and arrived at the Hautz home at the same time as the doctor. She broke down in tears at the sight of her dying son, cradling his head in her arms and asking him to tell her what had happened. "George shot me, mother," he said softly. Police officers and concerned neighbors soon filled the tiny room. The look on the doctor's face told the grieving mother that her oldest child was beyond help. Suddenly, William became alert, and he stared at the roomful of faces. "I'm going over," he declared before drawing his final breath.

After Dr. Stutzman pronounced William dead, his body was released to Undertaker Dreisebacher by Deputy Coroner David Hawk, who concluded that William had died from an internal hemorrhage caused by a punctured lung. He would be laid to rest at the family plot at Sacramento Cemetery.

According to relatives, George had been out of work for three years. He was the youngest of five brothers and two sisters born to William and Agnes Wessner and was regarded as the black sheep of the family, preferring to spend his free time roaming the hills and forests. George was not a physically imposing presence by any means; standing just five feet and four inches, he was described as being on the "wimpy" side, having wild, bushy brown hair and a nervous condition that made him blink uncontrollably whenever he spoke. He walked with a limp on account of a mining injury he suffered as a teenager.

Earlier that fateful evening, William had gone next door to visit his brother Harry, where the two men had discussed their younger sibling's inability to find a job. According to Harry Wessner, George had always been touchy on the subject of being unemployed.

By nightfall, a posse of twenty residents was searching the woods around Tower City, looking for the killer. The prevailing opinion was that George

Wessner had fled in a westward direction. Meanwhile, police investigated a report from across town that a gunshot had been heard near the swimming dam. Thinking that George might have taken his own life, authorities searched the area along Wiconisco Creek but found no trace of the fugitive.

In the morning, the search was aided by ten State Police troopers who focused their search on Peters Mountain and Clark's Valley, where they believed the killer was hiding, possibly near the home of his sister. A search party also went to Goldmine Gap to check on a hunting shack owned by the Wessner brothers, but no clues of recent habitation were found. Police widened their search to include the Pottsville and Pine Grove areas. Police as far away as Frackville were placed on alert after an overnight theft of two blankets from an automobile occurred there, leading police to wonder if the fugitive planned to stockpile supplies and provisions. Later that afternoon, the swimming dam was drained in connection to the suicide theory, but the body was not found.

The search dragged on for weeks, and the weeks turned to months. By summer, State Police had investigated dozens of George Wessner "sightings" throughout Schuylkill and Dauphin counties but could not prove that the man seen by witnesses was the same man who had shot and killed William Wessner. Another large posse was formed in July after William Wert, a farmer from Millersburg, reported a suspicious young man in ripped and tattered clothing crossing his field. Fishermen also saw the same man along Little Wiconisco Creek, and a man fitting the same description had also knocked on the door of and elderly woman, Mrs. Mary Dressler, seeking shelter for the night. This ragged wanderer was also seen a week earlier prowling around the woods of Armstrong Valley. The following month, a group of men hunting for groundhogs near Rife came across a vagabond sleeping atop a pile of hay inside an abandoned barn owned by Hiram Landis. Believing the man to be Wessner, they notified Officer Albert Hartman of Millersburg, but the vagrant was gone by the time he arrived.

THE HUNTED BECOMES THE HUNTER

In November, the best chance of apprehending Wessner came when the killer's sister, Lucy Shaffer, informed authorities that she had shot at a man who resembled him. The man had been attempting to enter the home in

Upper Clark's Valley through a window when he was discovered by Mrs. Shaffer, who aimed with her rifle. She told police that she found blood outside the house, leading her to believe that she had wounded the intruder. When they arrived on the scene, they followed the trail of blood to a swamp, but the direction of the trail suggested that Wessner had headed toward the mountains. For the first time in ten months, it appeared that William Wessner's slayer would soon be captured. With the weather turning cold and the fugitive presumably injured and in need of medical attention, Tower City was buzzing with gossip about Wessner's imminent arrest.

Less than one month later, on December 18, the Shaffer home burned down under mysterious circumstances. Police ruled it a case of arson, and the light of suspicion immediately fell upon George Wessner. Had the fire been set as an act of revenge against his sister for shooting him? Detectives believed this was the case. However, once again, the out-of-work miner managed to elude his pursuers.

After the fire, Lucy and her husband, John Shaffer, sought shelter in a Tower City apartment owned by John Peiffer. But things took a shocking turn the following morning when the apartment mysteriously erupted in flames around six o'clock in the morning. Only the quick response from the Tower City and Williamstown fire departments prevented the home's destruction. It now seemed clear that George Wessner would stop at nothing to get revenge against his sister. But while this made him a dangerous criminal, it also confirmed the assumption that Wessner was nearby, lurking in the shadows.

A SMALL MAN AT LARGE

Despite his habit of hiding in the vicinity, Wessner continued to baffle both local and state authorities. The search for the Tower City fugitive dragged on, much to everyone's amazement. Hundreds of strong, brutish mountain men had attempted to flee from justice in the wilds of Pennsylvania, only to be captured at the hands of lawmen. How, then, could a wispy, limping wimp like George Wessner survive for so long in the rugged mountains of Schuylkill and Dauphin counties?

In September of 1930, more than a year after the murder of William Wessner, the Homicide Division of the State Police asked for the cooperation of the Pottsville Police Department, who now believed that Wessner was being shielded by friends who lived there. Wanted posters were displayed throughout the city, but once again, the trail led to a dead end.

By the following February, not long before the second anniversary of William's death, the hopes for a capture—which had once seemed all but guaranteed—appeared to crumble. Was George Wessner alive or dead? Had his friends been able to transport him to a different state, where he found a new life with a new name? Or had he frozen to death on a cold winter night in a lonesome mountain cave? Were his bones rotting away at the bottom of some abandoned mineshaft? Or was it possible that he was still in the vicinity, somehow able to go about his daily life without arousing suspicion? Perhaps he had changed his identity, or perhaps he had a sibling or two who sympathized with his plight, a relative who took it upon himself to hide the fugitive until the heat died down.

A warrant charging George Wessner with murder was still in the hands of Leroy Kopp, the chief of police of Tower City. Would it ever be served?

THE END OF THE SEARCH

The answer to this question is a resounding "no." Despite the efforts of the State Police Homicide Division's best detectives and dozens of police departments, George Wessner was never found. It was as if the earth had swallowed him up completely—and, considering the number of coal mines in Schuylkill County—this might not be an exaggeration. This was the conclusion of many folks who lived in the area, though no evidence has ever been found to support this theory.

In May of 1937, Judge G.E. Gangloff of the Schuylkill County Orphan's Court declared George Wessner legally deceased for the purpose of settling the family's estate. While this ruling brought some closure to the Wessner family, it did not let the killer off the hook entirely; Gangloff explained in his ruling that Wessner could be tried on the murder charge in the event of his subsequent return to society.

While this never happened, it might have played out as one of the strangest events in the history of Pennsylvania crime; since the death penalty was in effect, George Wessner could have potentially been the first person to be executed *after* being declared legally dead.

9.
THE STRANGE CONFESSION OF LEOPOLD ROWE
(LEBANON COUNTY)

In July of 1893, murder was the hot topic of conversation around Lebanon County. On the morning of July 6, in the tiny North Dakota town of Cando, just south of the Canadian border, a family with local roots was horribly slaughtered. Fifteen years earlier, the Kreider family had left their home in Lebanon County for the frontier, taking with them a distant relative from Campbelltown to work as a hired hand on their North Dakota farm. This man, Albert Bomberger, killed Daniel Kreider and his wife, along with their five children, before being captured in Manitoba. On Tuesday, July 11, the bodies of the Kreider family arrived in Elizabethtown by train and, the following day, were laid to rest in one huge grave at Risser's Mennonite Meeting House cemetery in Mt. Joy Township (Barbara Kreider, the slain wife, was the daughter of John Risser). The funeral, which is believed to be the largest ever held in Lancaster County, drew between eight and ten thousand mourners, many of whom had been friends and acquaintances of the Kreiders during their time in Lebanon County.

Because of the sensational nature of the Kreider murders, not many people took notice of another murder, which was discovered near Campbelltown while Lebanon County was buzzing with gossip about the horrific slayings on the prairie. On the afternoon of July 10, just as the train carrying the corpses of the Kreiders was chugging into Pennsylvania, Coroner Reager of Lebanon County received a telegram requesting him to come to Palmyra to hold an inquest over the badly-decomposed remains of a man who was found dead beneath a haystack on a farm.

NEW YORK FATTY

Farmhand Edward Bachman was loading a hay wagon on the farm of S.F. Engle, on the road between Palmyra and Campbellstown, when he lifted a bale from a pile and stared into the unseeing eyes of a corpse. The head of the dead man was covered with vermin; the farmhand's shouts soon attracted a large crowd. The coroner arrived in mid-afternoon, and his examination of the remains revealed two bullet holes in the left temple. The dead man was a large fellow of about thirty years of age, heavy in build and six feet in height, clad in brown trousers, a white shirt and a vest, though his shoes were missing.

The coroner immediately concluded that the man had been murdered, and the body dragged about one hundred feet into Mr. Engle's field. There was no proof of identification and no clues to lead authorities to the murderer. With nothing more to go on than statements from locals, it was eventually believed that the victim was a German tramp known throughout the vicinity as "New York Fatty." The victim's real name was unknown, though some said that it might have been Shaeffer and that the man might have had connections in Wilkes-Barre.

Physician M.B. Fritz, upon examining the corpse in Palmyra at the direction of Coroner Reager, issued the following statement:

Palmyra, Pa., July 10, 1893. I, the undersigned, duly sworn by the Coroner, on the above date, do declare and say that the said corpse, unknown to any jury or community at large, has been murdered, to the best of my belief. I find on the left side of his head over the temporal region, two fresh stabs, also two bullet holes in the same region, the effect of which was sufficient to cause his death. Otherwise there were no scars or bruises on his body.

The coroner, upon returning to Lebanon on the seven o'clock train, notified the county almshouse and instructed the body to be brought back for burial. At three o'clock in the morning, the body arrived and was interred at the almshouse potter's field with little fanfare. Detective George Hunter conducted an investigation, but no clues were found, and the murder at the Engle farm quickly faded from memory.

THE TRAMP'S CONFESSION

On February 20, 1900, a tiny, hot-tempered, middle-aged German tramp found himself confined to a steel cell in the basement of the Lebanon city hall. He had been brought to Lebanon from the Berks County jail, where he had been picked up on a vagrancy charge. This was nothing out of the ordinary for 50-year-old Leopold Rowe, who had been drifting from town to town for the past ten years of his life. Rowe was no stranger to county jails and small-town lockups, and, under normal circumstances, he would've been out on the streets in a day or two after serving his routine vagabond sentence. But this time, things would be different. This time, Leopold Rowe admitted to being something more than a neighborhood nuisance or a petty thief—he admitted, on February 18, that he was the one who had slain New York Fatty in a farmer's field in Lebanon County seven years earlier.

Of course, there are many reasons why a habitual miscreant would cop to committing an offense that occurred in another jurisdiction. Sometimes, the quality of food is better in one county jail than in another, and sometimes, a prisoner has a pal locked up in another county whom he wishes to be reunited with. In the case of Leopold Rowe, however, it appeared that he had been brutally mistreated by the other inmates at the Berks County jail, and it was reported that Rowe's stay in Reading had been so miserable that he had attempted suicide.

From his cell in Lebanon, Rowe denied these accusations. No, the reason he had confessed to killing a fellow tramp was because he had been tormented, day and night, but the ghostly vision of his victim's face. When visited in jail by reporters, the self-styled murderer claimed that the image of his victim was constantly before his eyes, giving him no rest. It mattered not that Rowe's confession might send him to the gallows; he urgently needed the relief that a confession could bring. "I have trouble," Rowe moaned painfully, rubbing his temples. "My head hurts me," he said before he told his tale to Detective Sattazahn and newspaper reporters.

On the night of February 18, Rowe asked the night guard, Edward Koch, to come to his cell. When Koch obeyed, Rowe told him that he, along with a fellow tramp known only as "Yockey," had committed the foul deed on the road between Palmyra and Campbellstown in 1893. After Rowe pulled the trigger, the tramps had robbed the corpse of $50 before crossing the Susquehanna River and concealing themselves on a farm.

Normally, one would've scoffed at the notion—standing just 4'6" and weighing a mere 128 pounds, Leopold Rowe looked more like a gnome than a cold-blooded killer. But what made the confession believable was that Rowe knew every minute detail of the murder—not just the color and style of the clothing the victim had been wearing or the nature of the fatal injuries, but other details that had never made it into print. Warden Kintzer and Berks County officials looked into the matter and concluded that Rowe was probably telling the truth. He was transferred to Lebanon County by Berks County Sheriff Frank Brobst, and District Attorney McCurdy reopened the case of the Engle Farm corpse.

Leopold Rowe, however, didn't stick around long enough to wait for the conclusion of the investigation. Just hours later, after telling his story to the detective, Rowe wove a rope from strips of his bedsheets and hanged himself. Perhaps because of the impropriety of burying Rowe in the same potter's field as his purported victim, the almshouse steward, John Light, decided to ship Rowe's body to the University of Pennsylvania medical school in Philadelphia.

THE RAMBLINGS OF A MADMAN?

After a photograph of Leopold Rowe appeared in the *Reading Times*, former Reading Chief of Police Jacob Etzel recognized it as the likeness of a man who had been declared insane two years earlier before escaping from the Harrisburg State Hospital. While Berks County Detective Kershner admitted the similarity in appearance, however, he denied that Rowe and the escaped mental patient were the same man; the man who was committed to the asylum was named John Seifert, not Leopold Rowe. It was Etzel and Kershner, who was deputy sheriff at the time, who had conveyed the man to the asylum. To settle the debate, one journalist from the *Times* decided to investigate the matter and concluded that the tramp who had hanged himself in Lebanon after confessing to the 1893 murder was indeed the same tramp who had escaped from the Harrisburg State Hospital in June of 1897. But what was his real name?

On June 10, 1897, a man going by the name of John Seifert was arrested in Berks County by Chief of Police Albrecht at the request of farmers, who accused him of being a general nuisance. While locked up at the city police station, Seifert exhibited signs of insanity and a petition was presented to the court for the appointment of a lunacy commission. Judge Ermentrout appointed attorney Fred Hartgen, alderman E.S. Kirschman and Dr. Charles Haman to evaluate the tramp's mental condition. The report of the commission was filed on June 15, finding Seifert to be of "unsound mind" and recommending that he be committed to the state lunatic asylum. According to the report, the prisoner showed signs of extreme violence, having torn the steam heating pipes from his cell and smashing his bench into splinters.

On the morning of June 16, 1897, Seifert was transported from Berks County to Harrisburg. He spoke only in German during the trip and was so delusional that he believed that he was back in the old country, on the road to Bomberg. Physicians at the asylum pronounced his case a mild one; as a result, John Seifert (Leopold Rowe) was given minimal supervision, thereby giving him an opportunity to escape, which he did twenty-three months later, on May 9, 1899.

Whether Leopold Rowe was actually the man who had killed New York Fatty or was merely an unfortunate sufferer of mental illness who happened to learn the story from a fellow tramp before confessing it innocently as his own deed, will most likely never be known.

10.
GRANDPA ON THE GALLOWS
(LEBANON COUNTY)

Lined with quaint shops and historic buildings, Annville is one of the most charming towns in the Lebanon Valley. However, in 1887, Annville became the scene of horror after William Showers committed two of the most sensational murders in the county's history on the outskirts of town.

A cigarmaker by trade, William Showers lived his entire life in the Annville area. When the Civil War broke out, he enlisted in the Third Artillery, Battery II, but his military career was cut short after he was kicked in the chest by a horse. Upon his return to Lebanon County, he entered the cigar manufacturing business, which he conducted out of his home—a one-and-a-half-story log house on seven acres—on land that he had purchased from Samuel Harper (the namesake of the North Annville Township establishment known as Harper's Tavern).

William Showers had four children—Sarah, William, Stephen and Thomas. Sarah, who did not have the best reputation, was described as a "woman of questionable virtue" and had six illegitimate children. She finally married a man named Huffnagle, a rough character who had his troubles with the law, but Sarah passed away shortly after Huffnagle abandoned her and the children. Homes were found for all but two of them—Samuel Sperraw, age 3, and Billy Kahler, age 5.

Naturally, the duty of caring for these children fell upon William Showers, who, at the age of 60, was a widower and had neither the means nor the energy to accomplish this task. He was a cruel and demanding father, but he persevered. As a deacon in the local Lutheran church, he had a reputation to uphold. Nonetheless, he chafed under the additional expense this arrangement caused him. His business wasn't exactly thriving, and his army pension was scarcely sufficient to meet his most basic needs. He attempted to hire a housekeeper, Elizabeth "Betsy" Sargent, but the woman, after meeting the rambunctious toddlers, flat-out refused. She said that she'd only agree to the arrangement if the children were out of the picture.

Before long, William began to display hostility towards his grandsons. But then he had an idea. During those days, it wasn't unusual for young children to be "bound out" by parents or guardians who could not afford to take care of them. Under this arrangement, the children went to live in a new household, where they would eventually learn a trade as apprentices. When neighbors noticed that Samuel and Billy were missing, William explained that he had indentured them to a family from Tower City. But, while this practice wasn't unheard of, it was technically illegal (the federal government had banned indentured servitude 54 years earlier). This aroused suspicions that all was not right, and word eventually reached county officials in Lebanon. On May 31, 1887, Constable Fegan went to the Showers home and arrested him on suspicion of murder.

With William Flowers safely behind bars, authorities were able to make an investigation without fear of anyone hiding or destroying evidence. In jail, Flowers gave wildly conflicting stories: The children had been taken away by a man from Texas, they had been kidnapped by gypsies in the vicinity of Indiantown Gap, they had been given to a farmer in Tower City. He swore up and down that he did not know the whereabouts of Samuel and Billy, and tears streamed down his cheeks as he invoked the Lord to strike him down if he wasn't telling the truth.

SEARCHING FOR THE BODIES

The following day, District Attorney A.W. Ehrgood and County Detective James Gates left Lebanon in a buggy for Annville to assist in the investigation. By the time of their arrival, nearly every section of property had been searched for signs of freshly turned soil, and the searchers were growing discouraged. The Union Water Works dam was also dragged that afternoon. When Detective Gates learned from a nearby potato farmer that he had seen lights near a drainage ditch about 70 yards from the log house a few nights earlier, he instructed the men to search the ditch.

It was Frank Gruber who poked at the sandy bottom of the ditch with a stick and found what appeared to be human hair. He called out to the other searchers, and after a little excavation, the bodies of the two missing children were found about eighteen inches under the sand. Within minutes, word had traveled around town that the children had been found. Men and women crowded the ditch as the unclothed bodies, in an advanced state of decomposition, were pulled out of the sand and carried into the Showers barn.

Dr. I.K. Urich and Dr. John Bucher made a closer examination of the bodies of Samuel Sperraw and Billy Kahler inside the barn. Their bodies were blackened from a combination of sand and decay, their torsos bloated, and their eyes and tongues protruded. It was evident that the skulls had been crushed. A rope was found around Billy's neck. Even the sturdiest of the local farmers wept at the sickening sight. Others called for Showers' head. Next, authorities searched the house and found irrefutable evidence that a gruesome deed had been committed. The children's bed revealed faded blotches of blood—evidently, Showers had tried, in vain, to scrub away the telltale clues of his crime. Blood was also found outside the house. Not a stitch of the children's clothing was found, leading to the belief that they had been burned.

Upon interviewing neighbors, authorities believed that William Showers had killed his grandchildren out of his desire to get Betsy Sargent to marry him. William's wife and daughter had both passed away recently under suspicious circumstances, and it was hinted that William might've played a role in their deaths. It was also learned that Showers had tried, unsuccessfully, to have the children taken by the county almshouse and the Loysville Lutheran home. Authorities believed that, when these plans failed, Showers began to entertain the thought of murder.

Because the coroner was late in arriving, District Attorney Ehrgood instructed Justice of the Peace Isaac Beaver to hold the inquest. The jury assembled in the front room of the Showers home and proceeded to take testimony from witnesses who described Showers' recent movements and travels. Drs. Bucher and Urich both expressed their opinion that the boys had been bludgeoned over the head with a blunt instrument before being strangled. The jury fixed the date of the murders as May 17, 1887. This was the day the boys were last seen alive.

Owing to the advanced state of decomposition, Samuel Sperraw and Billy Kahler were buried in a hastily dug grave at Evergreen Cemetery on the night of May 31. It was a dark, starless evening and raining persistently. No weeping relatives or grief-stricken friends surrounded the simple pine coffins as their bodies were consigned to the earth. Meanwhile, a reporter from the *Lebanon Daily News* visited the accused killer in his cell on the upper floor of the county jail. Showers appeared haggard and feeble. He was unwilling to answer questions, though he declared that he was innocent.

On June 3, the murder weapon—a bloody hatchet—was found in Showers' outhouse, along with a blood-stained quilt. A few days later, Showers was moved to a new cell—Cell No. 13—so that guards could keep a close eye on him should he decide to take his own life before his case went to trial. Ironically, a former occupant of this very same cell, Nimrod Spattenhoover, was hanged for murder eight years earlier.

SHOWERS CONFESSES, IMPLICATES SARGENT

Over the summer, Showers' attorney, Col. A.F. Seltzer, tried every possible trick to aid his client, who maintained his innocence. His attempt to prove that Showers had a mental illness had gone nowhere, and the note Showers had produced—allegedly sent from a Tower City man offering to take in the two young children—was proven to be a forgery. Perhaps aware that his defense was going nowhere, Showers created a sensation on the morning of September 23—the date set for his preliminary hearing—when he called for his sons, Stephen and William, to visit him in jail so that he could make a full confession.

According to Showers, he and Betsy Sargent were engaged to be married (a claim which Sargent fervently denied), but Sargent desperately wanted William's grandchildren "out of the way." Together, in May, they concocted a plot to murder Samuel and Billy. On the night of the murder, Betsy held the lantern while William strangled the children—one with a length of twine, the other with Betsy's petticoat—and assisted him in burying the bodies in the drainage ditch. Showers claimed that the skull fractures occurred when he tripped and dropped the dead children. Betsy then stripped off the bloody clothing and burned them atop the kitchen stove.

When this confession was read in court later that morning, Betsy Sargent cried out, "That's a lie!" and she was removed from the courtroom by the order of Judge McPherson. While this outburst was dramatic, it was unnecessary because most educated people know that dead bodies can't bleed. Shortly after death, gravity draws the blood to the lower extremities in a process known as *livor mortis*—a fact apparently unknown to Showers. This could only mean that the victims had been bludgeoned while they were still alive. Nonetheless, defense attorney Seltzer appealed to the judge to have his client's guilty plea withdrawn. Judge McPherson ordered Betsy Sargent placed in jail while an investigation could be made. Sargent, from the confines of her jail cell, insisted that she could prove her whereabouts on the evening of May 16. She was soon released.

THE MURDER TRIAL

Showers' attorney, Col. Seltzer, immediately petitioned the court for a change of venue when the trial opened on the morning of December 15. The motion was denied. Also quashed was his petition challenging the jury selection. When Showers was led out of the courthouse that afternoon, he was hounded by a jeering crowd calling for his hanging.

The second day opened with a packed courtroom, with most of the attendees coming from Annville. Among the crowd was Betsy Sargent, who told reporters that if Showers were convicted, she'd gladly volunteer for the job of executioner. By late afternoon, the jury had been selected. The defense tried to prove that it had been "Cowboy" Huffnagle, Sarah's deadbeat husband, who had murdered the children and hid the bodies on the property to implicate Showers. Witnesses, including the accused killer's son and daughter-in-law, testified that the blood found on a cushion in the bedroom had been from a nosebleed. Other witnesses for the defense testified that Showers' confession had been made under duress amid threats by law enforcement.

As one might expect, it did not take long for the jury to find William Showers guilty of two counts of murder in the first degree. The verdict was read at eight o'clock on the morning of Sunday, December 18. Three ballots were taken; the first ballot produced ten votes in favor of the first degree and two votes in favor of the second degree. The second ballot went nine for the first degree and three for the second, while the third ballot found all twelve jurors agreeing on murder in the first degree. Col. Seltzer's motion for a new trial was dismissed on January 4, 1888, and Judge McPherson pronounced sentence, ordering Showers to hang from the neck until dead. Governor Beaver fixed the date of execution at November 14.

THE EXECUTION OF WILLIAM SHOWERS

Just after nightfall on November 13, 1888, Joe Bentz, the assistant janitor at the courthouse, brought the old scaffold out of the cellar. It was on this very scaffold the infamous "Blue Eyed Six" were hanged for the 1879 murder of Joseph Raber. Before long, a crowd of some two hundred people had gathered in the alley to watch George Hoffman and Adam Lutz erect the death machine on the south side of the jail yard, even though the execution would not occur until morning.

A little after seven o'clock the following morning, Showers ate a hearty breakfast of eggs, beefsteak and sweet potato in silence before combing his hair and spending his final moments reading his Bible. At 9:45 he was visited by Reverend Heil. Afterward, when he was handed his coat, he complained about it being dusty and demanded that it be brushed. Perhaps there was a reason why he wanted to look sharp; Betsy Sargent had expressed a desire to see the old man one last time. Though she set out for Lebanon, she didn't reach the prison in time, but before his execution, Showers exonerated her from any involvement in the murders.

At 10:25, the main doors were opened for those with admission cards to the hanging, but a bullrush ensued, forcing Deputy Sheriff Gerberich to block the entrance. Those who could not get inside took positions on nearby rooftops on Walnut Alley. Showers wore a black suit to the gallows, with a small bouquet of chrysanthemums in the left lapel, which had been placed there by Col. Seltzer, who accompanied him to the platform. Showers was stoic during his death march and expressed little emotion when the rope was placed around his neck and his arms and legs were pinioned. Only when Sheriff Yordy leaned in close and said goodbye did the condemned man begin to twitch involuntarily.

"Do you have anything you wish to say?" the sheriff asked, to which the condemned man replied that he had already said all that he had to say. The sheriff stepped down from the platform at 11:07 and sprung the trap. Showers fell with a thud, and Dr. Beckley pronounced him dead seventeen minutes later, death having been caused by strangulation. It was a fitting end for the man who had strangled his grandsons.

Neither of William's sons came to claim the body after the execution, which forced Sheriff Yordy to turn it over to Jacob Boger, steward of the county almshouse. However, Col. Seltzer, who was aware of his client's wish to be laid to rest alongside his wife, immediately went out in search of the dead man's sons to implore them to take possession of the corpse. He found Stephen at work in Christian Maulfair's stone quarry, though Stephen declared that he wanted nothing to do with the matter. Next, Seltzer tracked down William Jr. and urged him to claim the body, but he said that he didn't have the money to give his father a proper burial. Overhearing this, William's friends became so outraged that they hounded him until he reluctantly agreed to ask Undertaker Miller to fetch the body from the almshouse.

The body was immediately conveyed to Evergreen Cemetery, where a grave had been dug in the meantime, and Showers was buried alongside his wife in the same plot in which his murder victims—his very own grandchildren—had been buried. And so ends the final chapter of the history of William Showers, whose arrest, trial and execution created a deeper interest around Annville than any murderer who ever came before the Lebanon County court.

11.
THE MURDER OF AGNES COOPER WRIGHT
(DAUPHIN COUNTY)

On a warm, sunny morning in September of 1893, teacher David Beamsderfer stood in his one-room schoolhouse in Stoverdale, waiting for his pupils to arrive. It was a rare occurrence that classes began on time; many of the children had to walk a considerable distance through the woods and over the sandy hills south of Hummelstown to reach the schoolhouse. When the bell finally rang on the morning of Tuesday, September 19, Mr. Beamsderfer took roll call, noticing that one little girl was absent.

Agnes Cooper Wright had left her home in Derry Township at around seven o'clock that morning with her schoolbooks tucked under one arm and her lunch basket swinging from the other. To reach the school, nine-year-old Agnes had to walk two and a half miles along a hilly dirt road winding through a long stretch of dense forest. But Agnes knew a shortcut; about a half mile from the Wright home, there was a side path through a dark hollow. Though narrower than the main road and flanked on both sides by underbrush so dense it choked out the sunlight, this path would shorten Agnes' journey by a considerable length. The path would eventually come out at the road between Stoverdale and Round Top, which, to the casual observer, must've looked like a smoking volcano looming in the distance, thanks to the numerous charcoal furnaces which had been constructed there to provide the fuel for the local iron furnaces and limekilns.

At this point, where the side trail connected to the main highway, the lonesome road made a slight turn as if to swerve out of the way of the rugged nothingness that seemed to surround it on every side. It was here, in this seldom-visited spot, where a predator lay waiting in the shadows.

At 6:20 that evening, Arthur Cooper Wright arrived home from another exhausting day of work at Allen Walton's quarry, where he worked as a "scabbler," chiseling the blocks of brown sandstone for which Hummelstown was famous. Like many of Walton's top employees, Arthur Wright was a native of England, where he had learned the masonry trade. It was this abundance of English and Scots-Irish stonemasons that allowed Walton's Hummelstown Brownstone Company to produce some of the highest-quality building blocks in the world; by 1910, over 400 courthouses, mansions, churches and other buildings across the country had been constructed with blocks hewn from Walton's quarries. When his wife, Margaret, told him that Agnes had not returned home, Arthur was not overly concerned; it was not uncommon for the girl to visit her uncle's farm after school.

However, as it grew late, Arthur went to his brother's farm to fetch his daughter but was shocked to learn that she had not gone there. The Wrights spread the alarm to their neighbors, and a search party was hastily organized. Armed with lanterns, they scoured the woods and hills; they shone their lamps into the quarries and sand pits, wondering if the girl had stumbled in the darkness into one of the chasms. It was Barney Eisenhower, one of Arthur's co-workers from the Walton quarry, who finally discovered the body at around eight o'clock.

A BIASED SEARCH FOR AN UNBIASED MONSTER

Though just nine years old, Agnes Cooper Wright was unusually tall and attractive for her age. Although the identity of the killer had yet to be discovered, it was evident from the condition of the body just what his motive had been. The deep bruises on her thighs told the gruesome tale, as did the girl's underwear, which had been tightly knotted around her neck. The body was badly lacerated, proving that the girl had thrashed about madly in the thorny underbrush as she gasped for breath while her attacker strangled her. The body had been found about twenty-five yards from the main road, deep in the brush where the surrounding vegetation had been trampled flat, indicating that the killer had been waiting for his prey. Her books and lunch basket, along with her hat, were found across the road, leading authorities to believe that she had been ambushed and then dragged across the dirt path to the spot where she was violated and subsequently murdered. The men in the search party vowed on the spot that they would not wait for the law to bring the killer to justice—they would see to it themselves.

But who in the vicinity was depraved enough to commit such a fiendish act?

Upon learning of the death of Agnes Cooper Wright, newspaper reporters were quick to point the finger at one of the many Italian and Hungarian immigrants or black laborers who worked at the quarries. The thought that such an act could be carried out by a fellow with a good old-fashioned Anglo-Saxon name like Stansfield or Hawthorne seemed inconceivable; naturally, it had to have been the work of a foreigner or a black man. A reporter from the Harrisburg *Telegraph* raced to the scene of the crime the following morning, and the paper's editor, without any evidence, was quick to print the headline: *KILLED BY A HUN.*

Dozens of other Pennsylvania newspapers shared this anti-immigrant bias. The *Reading Times* wrote, "it is supposed the fiend who committed the crime was a Hungarian laborer," while the Lebanon *Daily News* went one step further and all suggested that the girl's killer might have been "a demented Hungarian" from Blair County who had been arrested in that city the day after the murder for carrying a knife in public. Throwing such things as evidence and probable cause out the window, the *Daily News* concluded its reporting by stating that the Hungarian man in question "should not be allowed to roam our streets when his few days' sentence has expired." The September 28, 1893 edition of the Carlisle *Weekly Herald* (which went into print after Agnes' non-Hungarian killer had already confessed to the crime) boldly printed the erroneous headline: *OUTRAGED BY A HUNGARIAN NEAR HUMMELSTOWN.*

Oddly enough, few of the papers demonstrating this anti-immigrant bias pointed out that the grieving parents of the innocent victim were immigrants themselves; however, the Lebanon *Daily News* did print a retraction of sorts the following day, stating that rumors of the crime having been committed by a "Hungarian or negro" were unsubstantiated.

When the body was discovered, Dr. W.C. Baker telegraphed the district attorney, Meade D. Detweiler, who immediately dispatched Detective Samuel J. Anderson and County Detective Spitler to the scene. Meanwhile, Coroner Hoy held an inquest at the Wright home that evening, with several neighbors called to testify. Hoy heard testimony from George Hoffen, Lizzie Hoffen, Lincoln Gardner, Abner Hummel, George James, Levi Manbeck, David Boyer, John Carmany, William Reigle and Mrs. Cooper, but none recalled seeing any strangers in the vicinity of Sand Hill that day. One possible clue came from the testimony of William Reigle, who said that Agnes Cooper Wright hadn't shown up that morning to pick up the two Reigle children on her way to school, as was her custom. This meant that Agnes had been attacked just ten minutes or so after leaving her house and that the killer had a head start of over twelve hours. If the killer were to be caught, the detectives would have to come up with a plan very quickly.

TENNIS THE TERRIBLE

Upon listening to the testimony given by neighbors, Detectives Anderson and Spitler were convinced that the fiend who had sexually assaulted and strangled Agnes Cooper Wright could only have been a local man. They turned their thoughts to local characters of less-than-stellar reputation, and one man in particular seemed to fit the bill. This suspect was an itinerant farm laborer named Benjamin Tennis. Illiterate, ill-tempered and impoverished, this fellow never seemed to be employed for any length of time and had been a thorn in the side of many of the families who lived in the vicinity. His wife having died a few years earlier and his younger children having been taken to the orphanage, Tennis no longer had a permanent address; his home was whatever dilapidated shanty he could find. He also knew the many paths and side trails around the quarries, which meant that he—unlike the immigrant laborers—was intimately familiar with the "lay of the land."

In order to track down the suspect, the detectives had to go undercover. Dressed as farmers and passing themselves off as day laborers, Anderson and Spitler went job hunting. On Thursday, September 21, Agnes Cooper Wright was laid to rest at the Wright family plot at St. Mary's Catholic Cemetery in Middletown, where the Wright family's handsome monument of Hummelstown brownstone still presents a striking contrast to the alabaster and marble slabs surrounding it.

Posing as farm laborers, detectives found Benjamin Tennis working as a corn cutter on the farm of Adam Strickler. They waited for an opportunity to confront the suspected killer, but this meant that, first, they would have to separate him from the deadly scythe he was holding in his hand. Luckily, this did not prove too difficult. It was evident to the detectives that Tennis didn't have much skill with the tool, and one of the detectives told Tennis that if he gave him the scythe, he would show him how to use it correctly. The ploy worked. After Tennis handed over the blade, the detectives introduced themselves and placed the suspect under arrest.

"I know nothing about the murder!" Tennis protested, though his skin had suddenly turned pale. "I didn't do it."

"Can you stand before the Redeemer and say you are not guilty?" demanded one of the detectives. At this, the suspect broke into tears.

"Yes, I did kill the little girl, but I didn't want to," sobbed Tennis as he was placed into a carriage bound for the Dauphin County jail.

During the trip to Harrisburg, Tennis spoke openly of his crime. He said that he had made frequent indecent proposals to the girl for several weeks at a spring near his home. Tennis, who was forty-three years of age at the time, lived with his two adult sons in a shanty about one hundred yards from the Wright family. Benjamin Tennis had gone so far as to nail boards over the Wright's well, thereby forcing Agnes to walk across Tennis' property in order to fetch water from the spring.

Agnes had stopped at the spring for a drink of water on her long walk to school on the morning of September 19. Benjamin Tennis was waiting for her. Taking advantage of the isolated location, he clapped his hand over her mouth and dragged her into a thicket by the roadside. His assault had caused her to bleed profusely; she had lost so much blood, in fact, that she was too weak to stand up, so Tennis stood her up against a tree in order to continue his despicable deed. The September 27, 1893 edition of the Lebanon *Daily News* describes what happened next:

Not being satisfied, he dragged her through the bushes and assaulted her again. All the while, she struggled heroically for her honor, but he overcame her. Little Agnes uttered these words, which no doubt cost her her life. "I am going to tell on you for this." Without another word, the villain took off her lower undergarments and, carefully wiping all the blood from himself, tied the same about her throat and strangled her to death.

According to Tennis, after murdering the girl, he immediately went to her uncle's farm and spent the afternoon whitewashing for Mr. Cooper. He was still at Cooper's farm when Arthur Cooper Wright came looking for his daughter later that evening. It was Benjamin Tennis himself who offered to put together a search party and go looking for her, which may help explain why he had managed to avoid arousing suspicion.

District Attorney Detweiler wasted no time bringing Tennis into court, where he was indicted by a grand jury on a charge of murder in the first degree. He pleaded guilty to the charge on the morning of September 27 before Judge McPherson, who had appointed David L. Kauffman and Robert B. Wallace as counsel for the defendant. There really wasn't much the defense attorneys could do; because Tennis had freely admitted his guilt, despite their instructions to the contrary, the trial would be little more than a formality. The judge remanded him to jail until the sentence was handed down, and everyone, including Benjamin Tennis, knew that the penalty would be death.

When Tennis was transported back to jail, he found a mob of two thousand angry men and women waiting for him. Although chants were calling for the killer's lynching, cooler heads prevailed, though, by all accounts, Tennis' night in cell number three on the ground floor of the Dauphin County Jail was an uneasy one. The gravity of the situation seemed to have hit him all at once. He requested a visit from his children, and his two adult sons, William and Joseph, were brought into the jail the following morning by Sheriff Buser. When Joseph Tennis asked his father if he had really committed the crime, he just replied, "Joe, I won't tell you anything now."

In the following days, knowing that his time among the living was short, Tennis requested visits from all seven of his children. This proved to be a logistical nightmare; because of the family's poverty, all but two of

Benjamin's children had been taken from his custody and placed in the care of Sand Hill neighbors over the years. The oldest child, Joe, was 21 but had been living with the family of Martin Ebersole. William, 19, and Dora, 17, were living with the Aaron Coble family. Benjamin, 14, made his home with John Tutweiler. Jerome, who was not yet old enough to work, was at the orphanage in Middletown. Sadie, 10, and the youngest child, Tommy, age 7, had been adopted by the family of John Rupp.

Tommy was the only child, apart from Benjamin's two adult sons, who visited the jail. John Rupp took Tommy to visit his father on September 28, but the seven-year-old boy had to be carried into the building kicking and screaming. He knew Mr. Tennis not as a father but as one of the many neighbors from the Sand Hill community. This made for an awkward meeting; when the little boy finally met his father, all he could say was, "Hello, Ben."

THE TURBULENT LIFE OF BENJAMIN F. TENNIS

The only possible chance Benjamin had of escaping the gallows was to be found insane, but even the killer's attorneys balked at this strategy. Benjamin himself scoffed at the notion, and both adult sons declared their father was perfectly sane. Yet, as the life story of Benjamin Tennis unfolded, some couldn't help but pity the pathetic figure whose remaining length of time on earth could be measured in days, not years. For some, Benjamin's plight served as a morality lesson; parents warned their children to go to school and work hard, or else they, too, might end up like the terrible Mr. Tennis.

Benjamin was born on the sand hills near Stoverdale on November 15, 1850. He was one of twelve children born to Samuel and Elizabeth Tennis. Seven of these children were already dead by the time Benjamin committed his vicious crime, and both parents had passed away decades earlier. Samuel and Elizabeth were very poor, and Benjamin was sent away to live with Samuel Keifer in Middletown at an early age, where he became an apprentice saddle-maker. This arrangement did not suit either party; Benjamin was not particularly bright or ambitious. He left Keifer's employ while still a teenager, and would spend the rest of his life hopping from farm to farm, performing any odd job or task that suited his meager ability. It was for this reason Benjamin never attended school and never learned to read or write with any degree of proficiency. Until the day of his death, he could not properly spell his name.

It was on one of these farms he met a young woman named Mary Bricker, and they were married by Rev. Joseph Nissley on December 26, 1872. The couple moved to Hummelstown and lived there until the birth of their second or third child, by which time their poverty necessitated a relocation to the sand hills, where they lived in a series of shacks and tumble-down shanties. Despite the financial hardship, Benjamin scraped together enough money to get by, but in 1888, his world was turned upside down.

In late November of 1887, there was a cave-in at the Walton quarry, which claimed four lives. One of the victims was Mary Tennis' brother. The body of John Bricker was the last of the bodies to be recovered; for over a month, it had been buried beneath tons of rock. John's body had been cut in half, and when the remains were brought home for burial on January 4, the sight of her brother's mutilated corpse was too much for Mary to bear. She collapsed while collecting alms for her family and died the following day.

Benjamin never recovered emotionally after the death of his wife, and Mary's sudden death left him with seven children to look after. One by one they were placed in the care of neighboring families, where they grew up unable to remember their early lives in the sand hills. As for Benjamin, he found himself living in a shack not far from the Wright family, lusting after little Agnes.

A NEW SUIT OF CLOTHES AND A BOXING KANGAROO

The notoriety of the crime turned Benjamin Tennis into a celebrity of sorts. Though forgotten or shunned by most of his children, there was never a shortage of visitors at the jail. One such visitor was John G. Foley, manager of the newly-built Eden Musee in Harrisburg, a turn-of-the-century amusement house featuring everything from lion wrestling and strongman exhibitions to comedians, freak shows, and wax dummies (it is worth pointing out that the Harrisburg amusement house was one of several Eden Musees owned by Harry Davis, the famous theatrical manager from Pittsburgh. It was Davis who first introduced the public to five-cent moving pictures, in the process coining the term "nickelodeon").

Foley visited the jail and gave Tennis a new suit in exchange for the clothes he had been wearing when he murdered Agnes Cooper Wright. The Harrisburg *Daily Independent* printed the contract between Foley and Tennis, which stated: *I hereby bequeath my clothing consisting of coat, pants, shirts, hat, shoes and stockings which I wore when I committed the murder to said John G. Foley, manager of Harry Davis Eden Musee for a consideration already received, viz: A new suit of clothes consisting of coat, vest, pants, hat, shoes and stockings.*

The contract was signed "Beng man f tennis," which were the only words the illiterate fiend ever learned to write. Foley promptly displayed the killer's outfit in the musee's "Curio Hall" as soon as the wax figure of the killer was complete, charging visitors five cents to view the ghastly spectacle or ten cents if they also wished to see the "marsupial pugilistic star," Dixon the Boxing Kangaroo, who was also on the bill that week. Contemporary accounts show that visitors were particularly interested in seeing Tennis's shoes, which still bore blood stains on them.

It was this new suit Benjamin Tennis wore into the packed courtroom on Friday, September 29, 1893. The first witness called was Agnes' mother, who sobbed hysterically during her testimony but whose testimony established a timeline of the murder. Subsequent witnesses corroborated Mrs. Wright's testimony, which included Coroner Hoy, Dr. Baker, William Reigle and his daughter Emma, Joseph Habershaw and Barney Eisenhower, the quarry worker who had found the body. A wave of anger rippled through the courtroom when Eisenhower described how Tennis had not only assisted in the search but had helped carry the wooden stretcher on which the body of his innocent victim was afterward removed from the woods.

The defense did attempt to raise questions about Benjamin's sanity, though it was evidently a lost cause. Witness after witness strongly rebuffed the notion of Tennis being insane. David Boyer, who lived across the street from the Wright family, shouted angrily at the defense attorney when he was asked if he had ever heard anyone refer to the defendant as "Crazy Ben." Tennis, who had already pleaded guilty, did not take the stand.

DAINTIES FOR A DEAD MAN WALKING

While Dauphin County waited for Governor Pattison to fix the execution date, the person who was growing the most impatient was the killer himself. In early October, Tennis told a reporter that he didn't want his execution put off for too long. "I get too tired to wait so long," said Tennis. "We must all die sometime, and I want it over as soon as they can get the thing ready."

On October 9, the governor fixed the date of the execution for Thursday, December 7. Sheriff Buser received the death warrant the following day and read it to the doomed man inside the office of Warden C.L. Brinser in front of several witnesses, including the killer's spiritual advisor, Rev. F.W. Staley. Tennis did not seem to care very much; he seemed in good spirits and didn't even flinch when the sheriff reached the part of the warrant stating, "and you shall be hanged by the neck until dead."

Benjamin had plenty of reasons for his good spirits. He had gained weight since his arrest and was eating better than he had at any point in his life. He wore the suit he had been given by the Eden Musee manager constantly, as it was the first set of new clothing he had ever owned. In jail, he got the first shave and haircut of his life and had his photograph taken for the first time. But Warden Brinser and the prison inspectors were most surprised by the gifts addressed to the convicted killer that kept rolling in. Two women had even shown up at the jail asking if they could present Tennis with a pound cake and cookies.

"I was so shocked I could scarcely believe that any person, much less a woman, would cater to the wishes of a man such as Tennis is, a man who committed the awful crime on little Agnes Cooper Wright and then murdered her," said one of the prison inspectors. "I thought, is it possible that a woman would lower herself to the extent of supplying such a villain with dainties? I told them to go and keep their presents and, rather, get on their knees and pray for the poor wretch. I do hope ladies will think better than to offer their compliments to this man. It is beneath the dignity of any woman to send presents to this man, and they should so consider it."

Of course, those were strange times. This was the era of curiosity seekers and relic hunters who trampled murder scenes in search of a souvenir, of men and women who paid a dime for the pleasure of staring at wax figures of Jack the Ripper, Lizzie Borden and Burke & Hare, a time when people forked over their hard-earned money to attend seances, to gawk at conjoined twins, to view the mummies of ancient pharaohs, or watch a man box a kangaroo. Not even the elites were above such macabre novelties and morbid amusements; on November 23, 1893, Dauphin County commissioner John Murphy was presented with a ghastly souvenir in the form of a cane made from the very tree against which Agnes Cooper Wright had been ravished before her murder.

On the morning of December 5, Benjamin was able to say goodbye to his three oldest children. Joseph, William and Dora were brought to the jail by Rev. Staley. For the first time since his sentencing, Benjamin wept openly. After joining his family in prayer, Benjamin presented his children with farewell gifts, purchased with the money he had received from his work on the Strickler farm. To Dora, he gave a box containing a Bible, in which Benjamin had underlined his favorite passages. To his sons he gave a tin-type photograph of himself, the only picture of Tennis that was ever taken. He instructed Joseph to make copies so that every one of his children could have a memento.

One particularly strange occurrence arose from the visit of Benjamin's children. One of the inmates, 45-year-old Cyrus Judson Neel, had caught a glimpse of 17-year-old Dora Tennis and had apparently fallen head over heels in love. He asked Benjamin for his daughter's hand in marriage, to which the latter replied, "You can have her to keep house and as your wife if you want her." After discussing the matter with Mrs. Brinser, the warden's wife, Dora politely declined the proposal.

JUSTICE WITH A SIDE OF STEWED OYSTERS

The gallows were erected in the jail yard near the west wall on Thursday morning. Only two passes had been handed out for the execution thus far, one to Arthur Cooper Wright and the other to his wife. This inspired hundreds of locals to take to the nearest rooftops and telegraph poles. Though the hanging would not take until the following morning, and it had been snowing since Wednesday, many curiosity seekers had already stationed themselves on their perches for fear of losing their lookout spot when the big moment finally arrived. From the upper floor of the courthouse, dozens of men, women and children looked out from the windows with morbid fascination as the heavy wooden death machine was erected in the jail yard. One remarked that he could clearly see the indentations in the upper beam from the rope used in previous hangings; others remarked that the scaffold had been given a fresh coat of paint for the occasion.

The morning of the execution dawned crisp and cold, and the promise of more snow kept the ghouls at bay. The treetops and telegraph poles had been deserted, and all was quiet outside the stone walls of the county jail. Benjamin Tennis appeared in good spirits, though he was disappointed to learn that he was not allowed to be hanged in his new suit. Still, he was cheered up to learn that he would be buried in it. For his final meal, he chose a breakfast of stewed oysters, sweet cake, and a quart of "the strongest coffee the cooks could make."

After breakfast, Tennis was moved to cell number twenty-three on the eastern side of the building so that he would be unable to hear the oiling of the gallows hinges and the testing of the trap door. This was just one of the many considerations Warden Brinser and his wife had made for the inmate. No matter how revolting his crime had been, the Brinser's deep religious beliefs compelled them to make the condemned man's final moments on earth as peaceful as possible. The warden had even gone so far as to smuggle some tobacco into the jail, which a Harrisburg newspaper reporter had provided. Although it was against the warden's own rules, he knew there was no harm in it. Justice would be served soon enough, and if a condemned man wanted to smoke a pipe before he was hanged, who was he to refuse?

In the killer's final statement to the press, he expressed his gratitude toward his captors. "I never thought you had such nice, kind people in Harrisburg as you have," said Tennis to a reporter from the *Daily Independent*. "Mr. and Mrs. Brinser were so good to me, and I hope to meet you and these good people in heaven." The thought of a man like Benjamin Tennis going to heaven made some of the prisoners and reporters laugh. Even one of the ministers on hand, Rev. Luther DeYoe, had to chuckle. He later told the reporter that Tennis ought not to be so certain about the final destination of his soul.

By eleven o'clock, the air had warmed considerably and, seemingly in the blink of an eye, hundreds of spectators had materialized on all sides of the jail. The ghouls had ascended to their rooftop perches once more, and local police had their hands full trying to keep the curiosity seekers at bay.

Many had followed Mr. and Mrs. Wright all the way from the train station, trying to sneak past the police and join the crowd of six hundred spectators who Sheriff Buser had granted access to the jail yard. The Harrisburg *Daily Independent* reported: Standing, sitting, pushing, this mass of humanity crowded around the scaffold, reciting incidents of other hangings they had witnessed and speculating on the execution of today.

At 11:19, Tennis was marched to the gallows, his spiritual advisors, Rev. Staley and Rev. DeYoe, by his side. His step was steady and strong, and he appeared not to be bothered by the taunts and jeers from the spectators. Standing alone atop the platform, he said, "I pray for all these people present, and I hope to meet you all when you die. I expect to go to heaven, and I want you all to come over. Now I come to the last when Jesus calls me home."

Deputies Keller and Roat, assisted by Ex-County Detective Geiger and Chief Clerk Smith, mounted the platform and pinioned Benjamin's arms. His hands were cuffed behind his back, and a heavy leather strap was tied around his ankles. The noose was lowered around his neck; a white cap was placed over his head. At exactly 11:30, Sheriff Buser pulled the lever and the trap was sprung. The body fell 34 inches, and after hanging for fifteen minutes, Benjamin F. Tennis was pronounced dead by the prison physician, Dr. Hartman. Coroner Hoy examined the body and noticed that the execution had been botched, perhaps in a karmic manner. The man who strangled Agnes Cooper Wright died not from a broken neck but from strangulation.

An immense crowd greeted the body at the railroad depot in Hummelstown when it arrived for burial. Nearly one thousand persons were on hand for the funeral of Benjamin Tennis, though only a handful mourned. Reverend Joseph Nissley read the 92nd Psalm as the body was lowered into a grave beneath a cherry tree at the northern end of the old Lutheran Cemetery.

12.

THE UNSINKABLE CORPSE OF JONAS SNYDER

(CARBON COUNTY)

In the spring of 1864, Union General Nathaniel Banks led an expedition up the Red River in an unsuccessful attempt to seize control of Louisiana, whose cotton fields were an important part of the Southern economy. Banks had 30,000 Union troops under his command, mostly from the Department of the Gulf and the Army of the Tennessee. Bolstering these infantry and cavalry divisions was the Mississippi flotilla of the US Navy, commanded by Admiral Porter, which consisted of ten ironclads, three monitors, eleven tinclads, and several smaller vessels.

One would not expect to find a boy from Carbon County among these forces, but in the spring of 1864, this is exactly where Jonas Snyder found himself. Snyder, who enlisted in 1861, left his home in Mahoning Township and joined the famous 47th Pennsylvania Infantry Regiment, which was composed primarily of young men and teenagers of Pennsylvania Dutch heritage from around the Lehigh Valley. Founded by Colonel Tilghman H. Good, the 47th Pennsylvania Infantry Regiment was comprised of ten companies. Company I, to which Jonas Snyder belonged, was the largest of these companies, with 102 men under the command of Captain Coleman Keck. Upon Keck's resignation in 1864, Company I was turned over to Captain Levi Stuber. Because it covered more miles during the war than any other regiment, the 47th Pennsylvania Infantry became known as "The Traveling Regiment." So, it is not surprising that Captain Stuber and his men found themselves in the Deep South as part of the Red River campaign.

The 47th Pennsylvanians arrived at Algiers, Louisiana, on February 28, 1864, and were then transported by rail to Brashear City before traveling by steamer to Franklin, where they joined up with troops from the Department of the Gulf's 19th Army Corps. With food and water in short supply, the 47th marched for weeks through New Iberia, Vermilionville, Opelousas and other towns en route to Natchitoches, which was their destination. After a brief encampment at Pleasant Hill on the night of April 7, the men began a particularly long and brutal march lasting from dawn to mid-afternoon of the following day, only to run headfirst into Confederate forces under the command of Major General Richard Taylor. The ensuing confrontation, known as the Battle of Sabine Crossroads, saw the 47th Pennsylvanians taking heavy casualties. But their suffering was far from over.

The next day, the 47th Pennsylvanians were ordered to form a defensive position on the Union's far right at Pleasant Hill. As the regiment's right flank spread out and up onto a bluff, they found themselves once again in the line of enemy fire. Although Banks' men eventually battled the rebels to a stalemate that day, the 47th once more suffered heavy losses. The regiment's second in command, Lieutenant Colonel George Warren Alexander, was seriously wounded during the fighting. Also wounded on Pleasant Hill was 65-year-old Benjamin Walls, the regiment's oldest member. Walls was gravely wounded while trying to prevent his regiment's American flag from falling into enemy hands (despite his injuries and being a wealthy farmer, Walls would attempt to re-enlist three years later at the age of 68).

As a result of the Battle of Pleasant Hill, the 47th became the first—and only—Pennsylvania regiment to have members held as prisoners of war at the notorious Confederate prison camp, Camp Ford. Sixteen members of the regiment made the grisly 125-mile march to Camp Ford in Texas. Two of these soldiers died in captivity, while another would die several weeks later at a Confederate prison in Shreveport.

Jonas Snyder was not among the sixteen Pennsylvanians taken prisoner, but the nonstop marching and fighting was beginning to take a heavy toll on his body. While records show that the 47th lost a total of 290 men during the war, only 117 died on the battlefield. Disease and illness claimed the lives of the other 173.

Surely, the young Dutchmen from the farmlands of the Lehigh Valley began to wonder if they would ever return home to their Hex-adorned barns and apple orchards; they wondered if they would ever again see the smiling faces of their mothers and fathers, sit down to a plate of *panhas*, or sink their teeth into a freshly-fried *fasnacht*. Pennsylvania surely must have seemed as far away as the moon when the 47th was ordered to fall back to Grand Ecore, where they remained until the end of April. And home became even more distant when the Pennsylvanians were forced to retreat further to Alexandria, with the enemy hot on their well-worn heels. On April 23, they managed to thrash Bee's Cavalry at Monett's Ferry, but the victory did little to buoy their spirits; by this time, most Union commanders had already given up the Red River campaign as a lost cause.

The month of May saw the 47th Pennsylvanians retreat across the Atchafalaya River, where they hoped to shield themselves from the pursuing rebels. On May 18, the final battle of the Red River campaign was fought at Yellow Bayou, where Banks' army was able to stave off a Confederate attack thanks to a forest fire ignited by both sides' artillery shells. Perhaps this was a miracle of sorts, for the fire allowed the Federal troops to flee to the safety of New Orleans, from where they would return to Washington, D.C., aboard the steamship *McClennan*.

It was shortly after the Battle of Yellow Bayou when Pvt. Snyder fell gravely ill and was placed in a military hospital in New Orleans. When the steamship *McClennan* left New Orleans on July 5, Private Jonas Snyder was aboard, along with other Union troops who had been convalescing in New Orleans, but as the ship crossed the Gulf of Mexico, Snyder succumbed to his illness. He was buried at sea.

It was Lieutenant James W. Stuber, a close friend of Jonas and brother to regimental commander Capt. Levi Stuber, who witnessed the funeral, recalled, many years later, a bizarre incident that occurred. As was often the case with sea burials, Snyder's body had been weighted down with iron before being placed in the water. Stuber watched the body go overboard and sink into the waters of the gulf until it had disappeared. Stuber wrote: "By reason of the under current it returned as it were, and stood erect and life-like upon the water, as if to say I want to go with you, then disappeared again."

Of course, there is probably a scientific explanation for what happened to the corpse of Private Jonas Snyder. Perhaps it was a freak occurrence of nature or a perfect combination of weight, buoyancy, water temperature, density, current, or any one of a hundred other natural factors. But one of the saving graces of war, especially a war so cruel as the one fought between the states, is its propensity to romanticize the dead long after the soldier has departed from the mortal realm, lest we forget about the sacrifices that were made and the brave men and boys who made those sacrifices.

And one could be forgiven if one chooses to view the "unsinkable corpse" of Jonas Snyder as some sort of supernatural phenomenon. After all, records indicate that every male member of the Snyder family, brothers and cousins alike, enlisted in the 47th Pennsylvanian Infantry. And all, except for one, made it back to the Lehigh Valley. So perhaps it is possible that what Lt. Stuber witnessed aboard the *McClennan* was one young soldier's last attempt to come home after marching countless miles across the deep South with the outfit of heroes known as "The Traveling Regiment."

13.

CYRIACUS SPANGENBERG: THE MURDEROUS MINISTER

(SOMERSET COUNTY)

The historical record shows that 1,043 criminals are known to have been executed in Pennsylvania, beginning with the hanging of Derek Jonson in Bucks County in 1693 and ending with the lethal injection of Philadelphia serial killer Gary Michael Heidnik in 1999. Of these 1,043 persons who paid the ultimate price for their crimes, many were gangsters, ex-convicts and career criminals. Several had unusual occupations; Lorenzo Savage, who was electrocuted in 1924, was a voodoo doctor, while William Rumage, electrocuted in 1948, worked for a circus. Lawrence County banana dealer Frank Jongrass went to the gallows in 1898, while jeweler John Bruelman was hanged in Philadelphia in 1760. But of these 1,043 men and women executed, only one was a clergyman—Cyriacus Spangenberg.

The story of Cyriacus Spangenberg begins during the time of the American Revolution, when hundreds of Hessian mercenaries arrived in this country to aid the British. Spangenberg came to America as a Hessian soldier but soon tired of the rigors of military life and settled in western Pennsylvania. A well-educated man from a respectable family, Spangenberg arrived in Philadelphia on May 14, 1783, seeking ordination in the Reformed Church. His uncle, Reverend Samuel Dubendorf, was an esteemed Reformed clergyman, and so one can imagine Spangenberg's disappointment when church leadership refused his ordination request. When the church once again refused to ordain him two years later, this time in Lancaster (amid concerns about his conduct as a soldier), Spangenberg turned to a friend of his uncle, a minister named Philip Jacob Michael. Reverend Michael ordained Spangenberg, and the former soldier immediately embarked upon a career as a preacher.

After preaching to congregations in Sunbury, Selinsgrove, Middle Creek, and Mahantango (Snyder County), Spangenberg returned west to the village of Berlin in present-day Somerset County sometime around 1788 and continued to preach there until 1794. However, by this time, revelations concerning his personal life came to light. It seems that while Spangenberg was a pastor of the Mahantango Reformed Church of Salem, he had intended to marry a local girl, but the day before the planned wedding it was discovered that Spangenberg already had a wife back in Germany. He fled Snyder County in disgrace, but word of his conduct eventually reached Berlin.

Cyriacus Spangenberg was the first resident pastor in Berlin, which is situated about seventy-five miles southeast of Pittsburgh, and he also served a number of other nearby towns, including Bedford, Saltsburg, and Stoyestown. When gossip about Spangenberg's adulterous behavior reached Berlin, a meeting of the church elders was held. This meeting, which took place on March 19, 1794, infuriated the former soldier, who was present during the entire assembly. Though Spangenberg had his share of supporters within the Reformed Church, he also had made a number of powerful enemies.

One such enemy was a 60-year-old elder named Jacob Glessner, who was regarded as a pillar of the church. Whether or not Spangenberg remained pastor was up to a vote of the congregation, and it appeared that Spangenberg had a good chance of keeping his position—that is, until Glessner stood up at the end of the proceedings and encouraged members of the congregation to vote in favor of the pastor's removal. Since Elder Glessner was a very influential member, this spelled doom for

Spangenberg. In a fit of rage, he drew a knife that had been concealed in his clothing and plunged the blade into the heart of Jacob Glessner. With blood gushing in torrents from his chest wound, Glessner fell at the foot of the altar and died.

The congregation was so horrified that they did not attempt to subdue or apprehend Spangenberg, who fled from the church and retrieved his horse from the adjoining pasture (this pasture was known for many years following the murder as the "Pfarrer Schwam," or "Parson's Swamp"). Once the congregation gathered their wits, they went off in search of the murderous minister, and he was soon found and arrested. After being apprehended by David Eshbaugh and Mathias Zimmerman, Spangenberg defiantly proclaimed, "*Ich habe nicht geduhn; mein Herr Gott hats geduhn* (I have done nothing; my Lord God has done it)."

Spangenberg was taken before the Berlin justice of the peace, Adam Miller, and committed to the Bedford Jail. Justice Miller's notes from the hearing indicate that the murder occurred at approximately two o'clock and took place in Spangenberg's living quarters, which were attached to the log church building. This, according to some, casts some doubt about Glessner falling dead at the foot of the altar, and in some versions of the story, Spangenberg called Glessner into his living quarters in order to have a word with him in private, where he was stabbed and died of his wounds two days later. This version, while slightly less dramatic, would seem to be the correct version, as the Grand Inquest indictment from the April 1795 term of court, signed by Attorney General Jared Ingersoll, states that "Jacob Glessner languished until March 21."

Regardless of which version of the stabbing is accurate, records show that Spangenberg's murder trial took place on April 27, 1795, in Bedford (Somerset County was still part of Bedford County at the time) and that he was found guilty of murder in the first degree and sentenced to death. His attorney attempted to secure a pardon through the governor, but the effort failed. On September 11, Governor Thomas Mifflin issued his warrant to Sheriff Jacob Bonnett directing the execution of Cyriacus Spangenberg to take place on Saturday, October 10.

On the day of the execution, the doomed preacher, with his coffin on the same wagon, was conveyed to the gallows. A large crowd gathered at the public square in Bedford to watch as the rope was placed around Spangenberg's neck, and the killer was hanged until he was dead. Unfortunately, the final resting place of Cyriacus Spangenberg is unknown, though the story of his crime is still a popular tale in Somerset and Bedford counties.

14.
DARK SECRETS OF THE EPHRATA CLOISTER
(LANCASTER COUNTY)

Located in Lancaster County, the historic Ephrata Cloister and its museum are visited by hundreds of tourists each year. Founded as a religious colony in 1732 by Johann Conrad Beissel, members of this strict religious community adhered to the principles of the Schwarzenau Brethren (or German Baptist Brethren), which date back to 1708, when Alexander Mack inspired his followers to break away from the Roman Catholic and Protestant churches of Germany. Driven out of the country by the established churches, the Brethren found exile in the Netherlands until 1719, when Peter Becker encouraged all but a handful to emigrate to Pennsylvania. By 1733, most of the Brethren had arrived in Germantown, near Philadelphia, and settled among the Mennonites.

One of the earliest of these arrivals was Conrad Beissel, who found that even the doctrine of the Schwarzenau Brethren was a bit too liberal for his liking. Upon his arrival in 1720, he intended to join the hermitage founded by Johannes Kelpius, the Transylvanian religious mystic who lived in a cave along Wissahickon Creek and preached that the world would end in 1694. Kelpius' movement lost much of its steam after his prophecy failed to come true, and Kelpius himself lost the rest of his steam entirely in 1708 when he died at the age of 40. This must've been quite a shock to his remaining followers since Kelpius had often claimed to be immortal (he also claimed to possess the so-called Philosopher's Stone, which allowed alchemists to not only turn worthless materials into gold but to achieve immortality; according to legend, Kelpius had lost his stone in the Schuylkill River, thereby explaining his seemingly-impossible death to his gullible followers). Kelpius was also an accomplished musician and author, which, in a way, kind of makes him one of America's first social media influencers.

In Germantown, Beissel earned his keep as a weaver's apprentice and struck up a friendship with one of Kelpius' former monks, Conrad Matthaei, and from the latter's settlement along Wissahickon Creek, they took turns staying awake and watching the skies for the eminent second coming of Christ, as Kelpius had foretold (astrology would later become a key component of Beissel's religious beliefs). Before long, Beissel had become disenfranchised by Matthaei and decided that it was probably more fun to be a cult leader than a cult follower, so he formed his religious order along Cocalico Creek in Lancaster County and laid the framework for what would eventually become the Ephrata Cloister.

But this period of Beissel's life was not without controversy. In 1726, six years before the Cloister sprang into being, while Beissel was building a cult-like following throughout Chester and Lancaster Counties, two young daughters—Anna and Maria Eicher—ran away from their father's house and placed themselves under Beissel's guidance after being mesmerized by his preaching. These living arrangements created much gossip throughout the community, and to prevent any possible scandal, the members of the congregation built a separate cabin for the two sisters, who became the first of Beissel's followers to adopt (perhaps against their wishes) the sort of monastic lifestyle for which the Cloister later became famous.

THE EARLY LIFE OF CONRAD BEISSEL

Beissel, it seems, had a long and complicated history with the opposite sex, which perhaps formed his later opinions on celibacy. His father, said to be a drunkard of low moral quality, died before Conrad was born. His mother raised him until her death left him an orphan at the age of eight. As a ward of the state, Conrad was apprenticed to a baker when he reached working age, and it was under the tutelage of this master baker he learned how to play the violin. Young Conrad frequently accompanied his master to parties and dances and soon gave up baking altogether to pursue his love of music—and women—full-time. Historian Julius Friedrich Sachse wrote of Beissel: *Being a comely youth, it was not long before he would rather fiddle at a wedding feast and turn a buxom damsel in the dance than knead his dough or rake the oven.*

According to Sachse, Beissel wandered throughout Germany learning the baking trade and eventually found himself in Mannheim, where he entered the service of a baker named Kantebecker. Sachse continues: *After remaining a time at Mannheim, he was forced to leave his master's house on account of some trouble with the latter's wife, whom he called a "Jezebel."*

It was around this time the young man had a religious awakening; within a few years, he would find himself in America, extolling to his followers the virtues of celibacy and forbidding the use of musical instruments at his religious services. From Germantown, he went to Berks County, Schuylkill County and Lancaster County, traveling from camp to camp with a dozen or so members of the German Brethren. Although he had been baptized in the Wissahickon by the Brethren (their fervor for baptism led to the label "Dunkers," which is still in use today), he felt that it didn't "take," and was later again re-baptized in Pequea Creek after he and his companions had splintered from the Dunker church. This second dunking seemed to do the trick, and before long, Beissel found himself the elected leader of his congregation. His companions from this time would later become Elders of his religious order.

CAMP OF THE SOLITARY

The colony founded by Conrad Beissel on Cocalico Creek in 1732, initially known as the "Camp of the Solitary," included a convent for the women and a monastery for the men, as well as a communal meetinghouse called the Saal. The charismatic Beissel, who had since changed his name to Friedsam, ruled over his colony with absolute authority, dictating every aspect of the members' lives; they were forced to sleep on narrow wooden benches with wooden blocks for pillows (Beissel abhorred birds and detested anything made from feathers, so pillows and blankets were off-limits), and they were limited to one vegetarian meal per day (meat was strictly forbidden except on Easter). Historian Edward Eggleston, in 1886, wrote of the reasoning behind Beissel's peculiar dietary restrictions: *He had forbidden all animal food. Not only was meat of evil tendency, but milk, he said, made the spirit heavy and narrow; butter and cheese produced similar disabilities; eggs excited the passions; honey made the eyes bright and the heart cheerful but did not clear the voice for music.*

The members promptly went to bed at 9:00 each night, with each member taking a two-hour shift to watch out for the coming of Christ. The members were expected to wear white robes, take a vow of celibacy, and spend their waking hours in prayer and physical labor. Even in death, members of his church could not escape his fanatical mandates; Beissel even had strict rules about how members of his congregation were to be buried.

In addition to his fanatical rules about food (the members' diet was primarily limited to buckwheat, cabbage, potatoes, turnips and fruit from the colony's orchard), Beissel even had strict rules about how his hymns were to be sung—Beissel alone wrote and composed the hymns, which were to be sung (no musical instruments were allowed) using a series of "master" and "servant" notes, in a minor key, which, when sung together, created a peculiar, ominous harmony. It also served as a subliminal method intended to reinforce Herr Friedsam's position as absolute ruler of his quirky, private kingdom.

Of Beissel's strict mandates concerning music, Eggleston writes:

Most of the songs sung in the little building called Zion were written by him . . . songs in praise of the mystical marriage of virgins with the chaste Lamb; songs about the Philadelphian brotherhood of saints (here Philadelphia refers to a mystical city of pure joy, a common theme in Beissel's teachings), about the divine Sophia (a celestial wise being about whom Beissel also preached), and about many other things which no man can understand, I am sure, until he has first purified himself from the gross humors of the flesh by a heavenly diet of turnips and spring water.

In his 1899 history of the German Brethren in Pennsylvania, author Julius Friedrich Sachse of Ephrata described Beissel's behavior shortly after being elected head of the congregation:

Beissel, in his addresses, now frequently introduced some of the mystic speculations of occult theosophy, which most of his simple-minded hearers failed to comprehend. The effect of this was that, while some of them deemed him inspired, others shook their heads sadly and thought him demented.

While historians are tempted to idealize the Ephrata Cloister as a utopian commune comprised of quiet, pious and industrious Christian vegetarians, the reality is that the Cloister was not much different than a prison camp and that Beissel was not much different than any other charismatic cult leader throughout history who imposed his strange whims upon a group of vulnerable people through methods of psychological manipulation (sleep and food deprivation, physical discomfort, celibacy, subliminal messaging, deprivation of medical care, etc.). Continual physical labor in a collective environment does wonders to discourage individual thought, and there was no shortage of work around the Cloister. Members were required to engage in carpentry, farming, operation of the printing press, and manufacturing of paper, furniture and clothing—very much the same industries one finds in a modern-day penitentiary or prison farm.

Historian Eggleston, who was also an ordained Methodist minister, was perhaps one of the earliest critics of Beissel's mind-control methods. Eggleston writes:

Their perfection of execution was attained at a cost almost too great. Brother Friedsam was a fanatic, and he was also an artist. He obliged the brethren and sisters to submit to the most rigorous training. In this, as in religion, he subordinated them to his ideals. He would fine-tune their very souls to his own key . . . At the singing school, Brother Friedsam could not abide the least defect; he rated roundly the brother or sister who made any mistake . . . if it is ever necessary to account for bad temper in musicians, one might suggest that the water-gruel diet had impaired his temper and theirs.

Like many radical religious leaders before and after, Beissel soon realized that celibacy was not a very good way of ensuring the long-term viability of his colony. Not only was it a lousy selling point for the recruitment of new members, but it limited the lifespan of the religious order to one's lifespan. By the early 1750s, membership had dwindled to less than a hundred celibate vegans, and Beissel remedied the situation by extending membership to about two hundred non-celibate "Householders," who occupied adjoining homes and farms who were invited to join in worship at the Cloister. They soon came to adopt Beissel as their spiritual leader, and this ensured the colony's survival until the death of the last celibate member in 1813, some forty-five years after the death of Conrad Beissel. After 1813, the members of the religious order were incorporated into the German Seventh Day Baptist Church, though religious services were conducted at the Cloister until its closure in 1934. The last surviving resident of the Cloister, Marie Kachel Bucher, passed away in 2008 at the age of 98.

Beissel, who died in 1768, is buried in the Ephrata Cloister Cemetery along with nearly three hundred of his followers and Householders, and a plaque at his gravesite (translated from German) reads: *Here rests offspring of the love of God, Friedsam, a Solitary, but later became leader, guardian and teacher of Solitary and the Congregation in Christ in and about Ephrata. Born at Eberbach in the Palatinate, called Conrad Beissel, fell asleep July 6th, anno 1768; Aged according to his spiritual age 52 years, but according to his natural, 77 years and 4 months.*

THE COLONY OF MISERY?

Many of the gravemarkers at the Cloister cemetery are excellently preserved, and these markers offer valuable insight into conditions inside the colony. A casual stroll through the old graveyard reveals the final resting place of an astonishing number of church members who failed to survive into middle age and a few who made it to old age. There are 240 gravemarkers in which both the birth and death dates of the deceased are inscribed, with the average age at the time of death being a mere 50.96 years. One might be tempted to say, "Well, life expectancy was shorter back then, so that's not unusual," but this does not explain why the age-at-time-of-death average seems to drop precipitously after the Brethren arrived in Ephrata.

This average age at the time of death is bolstered by a score of followers who survived to an age that is enviable even by today's standards. These deceased followers include: Johan Diedrich Fahnestock, age 79 (b. 1696), Joseph Heffley, age 80 (b. 1727), Salma Heffley, age 79 (b. 1727), Ludwig Hocker, 74 (b. 1717), Anna Magdalena Klopp, 76 (b. 1690), Johann Peter Klopp, 87 (b. 1686), Elisabeth Keller, 79 (b. 1708), Hans Jacob Keller, 87 (b. 1706), Anna Catarina Lassle, 94 (b. 1652), Sebastian Keller, 77 (b.

1729) Barbara Rohrbach, 86 (b. 1708), and Peter "Brother Jabez" Miller, 86 (b. 1709), who succeeded Beissel as leader of the community.

What do these people have in common? Well, for starters, they were all living during Beissel's lifetime and were not born inside the walls of the colony. Most had already reached adulthood before the Cloister was founded in 1732. If you subtract these early followers, this lowers the age of the typical Cloister member at their time of death to well under 50. You can also subtract the oldest person buried in the graveyard (Lydia Miller Konigmacher, age 96) because she lived in a stone mansion between Ephrata and Springville and never lived inside the Cloister. So why should the early followers who were born and raised outside of Ephrata live to a respectable average age of 83 years, while those who were born inside the Cloister only have a life expectancy of 49 years? That's a whopping difference.

What killed Orion Addams at the age of 23? How could it be that, out of the three Benjamin Baumans buried there, none survived past the age of 44? Why was George Gorgas only 24 when he died? What manner of death befell Henry Huber and Henry Hahn at the age of 13? Why did a man in the prime of his life like Michael Sensaman perish at 22? Or a man at the height of his vigor like Joseph Sensaman die at 24? Had there been a war going on at the time of their deaths, we might attribute the death to Confederate shells or British bullets—but there wasn't. In fact, none of the church members had served in the military (although taking up arms was against church teachings, the Cloister buildings were, in fact, used as a military hospital during the Revolutionary War after the Battle of Germantown).

How did Samuel Slough and Sarah Slough both die at 4 years of age? If there was an outbreak of scarlet fever or some other disease that swept through the colony, we might blame it on that . . . but they died ten years apart. In fact, it seems that the residents of Beissel's utopia were fairly well-protected against epidemics; during the outbreak years of scarlet fever (1858), typhoid fever (1906-1907) and the three major cholera waves (1832, 1849, and 1866), the Cloister Cemetery saw just eight total burials. If war and disease were not the culprits behind the overwhelming proportion of untimely deaths at the Cloister, then what was? One can only conclude that the Ephrata Cloister was not the quaint, lovely place romanticized by white-robed tour guides or the enterprising enclave mentioned in history books. The state can put up all the misleading historical markers it likes, but the reality could only have been this: Life at the Cloister was dreadfully harsh and short. It was less of a utopia and more of a hell on earth, where malnutrition, abuse and neglect ran rampant.

Proof of this can be seen when comparing the average age at the time of death at the Cloister Cemetery with the average of other nearby cemeteries of the same period. These burial grounds contain the remains of people of the same Palatinate heritage who lived in the same geographical region in Lancaster County at approximately the same time. Why should one vary so greatly from the others? For instance, by calculating the average age at the time of death from other nearby cemeteries, we can see that while the average at the Cloister Cemetery is 50.96 years, the average for the Gross Cemetery in Ephrata is 68.9 years, the German Reformed Church Cemetery (Strasburg) is 59.1 years, and the Dornbach Cemetery (Cocalico) is 56.95 years. Again, these figures are based upon only the gravemarkers which show a legible birth and death date.

One might be tempted to blame this discrepancy on stillbirths or infant deaths, but, not surprisingly, only a few infant deaths occurred inside a colony whose members were known for celibacy; by my count, I've found only four persons buried at the Cloister who passed away in the first few weeks of life. More infants are buried at the graveyards above than at the Cloister cemetery, which suggests that it was the young adult at the Cloister who suffered the most.

Of course, one should not hold Beissel entirely accountable for conditions inside the Cloister. The cemetery burials show that his original "brothers" and "sisters" who were born outside the colony enjoyed long, healthy lives. Upon Beissel's death, when the reins were handed over to Peter Miller—"Brother Jabez"—the members also continued to survive to an admirable age. However, in the decades following Miller's death, we see a dramatic shift in life expectancy. Inside the Cloister graveyard, we find the burials of 35 children under the age of ten, eight teenagers, 16 persons aged 20-29, and 19 persons between the ages of 30 and 39.

Skeptics may point out that not all burials at the graveyard were those of Cloister members and that the "Householders" who were buried there were prone to farming and industrial accidents. This is true, but of course, the same thing applies to other local cemeteries, where the majority of interments are also farmers and laborers. In fact, you'll find members of the very same families in the other burial grounds I've sampled, names like Bauman, Bucher, Fahnestock, Konigmacher and Zerfass. This would also exclude the possibility of a "hereditary taint" being the cause of the Cloister's premature deaths since the same maladies would affect the same families regardless of burial place.

THE EXHUMATION OF SOPHIA BAUMAN

It is well established that Beissel imbued his religious "society of solitude" with his unique brand of occult mysticism and superstition (In Germantown, Beissel had joined the secret society of the Rosicrucian Order, and historian Sachse writes of a "Brother Jephune" who served as Beissel's chief astrologer at the Cloister), and it has been written that Beissel's preaching was especially effective on the ignorant and simple-minded. One demonstration of the typical scientific ignorance and superstition that was rampant at the Cloister took place in 1743, with the passing of a comet, which Beissel heralded as an omen of destruction (it wasn't).

More than a century later, the residents of the Cloister demonstrated their primitive superstitions again with the gruesome exhumation of a woman whose death, according to some members of Beissel's church, was caused by supernatural forces.

On Sunday, May 24, 1857, the people of Ephrata were startled to learn that the remains of Sophia Bauman, who had died of consumption in 1850 at the age of 32, had been exhumed from the Cloister Cemetery by two men hired by the congregation. For the God-fearing residents of Ephrata, desecrating a grave on Sunday was a horrific thing, but since the Brethren believed that the true Sabbath was on Saturday (hence their designation as "Seventh Day Baptists"), those at the Cloister did not take offense at their neighbors being offended.

One newspaper correspondent from the Lancaster *Express* traveled the short distance to Ephrata to gather news about the strange exhumation and learned that since Sophia Bauman's death, two other sisters, two brothers and the mother had also died prematurely, presumably from the same disease. While local physicians were strongly of the opinion that the Bauman clan had all been stricken by tuberculosis, those at the Cloister pinned the blame on the old German superstition of the "winding sheet."

In traditional Orthodox Jewish and Muslim burials, the deceased is wrapped in a white shroud made of cotton or linen prior to burial (the Shroud of Turin is the world's most famous example of a winding-sheet). At one time, this custom was also popular with the early Christian church, though it had fallen out of favor by the end of the Dark Ages. However, since Beissel's theology was heavily influenced by Mosiac Law, members of his church were also wrapped in a winding-sheet prior to burial. According to a strange and outdated legend, if a portion of the burial shroud should find itself inside the mouth of the deceased, the surviving family members would be "sucked" into the grave, too. One newspaper account of the Bauman exhumation, from the Lewistown *Gazette*, stated:

The opinions of physicians were set aside by the incursions of ignorance and superstition, under which the belief was seriously entertained and acted upon, that by some hocus pocus, the winding sheet of the corpse had got into her mouth, and that by a continual suction (the modus operandi of which was only known to the spirits) she had actually drawn the other five members of the family after her, and unless this winding sheet was speedily removed from the mouth of the corpse she would, in like manner, cause the premature death of the whole connection . . . Incredible as a belief in such a monstrous superstition in this enlightened age may appear, it is nevertheless true, for according to previous arrangements, the resurrectionists commenced operations on Sunday morning.

Of course, the digging up of Sophia Bauman was in vain—not only was the burial shroud not inside the corpse's mouth, but the Cloisterers had overlooked the fact that most of the winding sheet, being of organic material, had rotted away years earlier. It seems the corpse was reburied, and the incident was never spoken of again.

Sadly, one can only feel sympathy for the poor, deluded folks who called the Cloister home, who toiled in labor and suffered in solitude and kept a constant eye turned toward the night sky for comets, shooting stars, and other portentous omens which their zealous leader, Conrad Beissel, assured them would foretell the coming of Christ. One can only wonder if many of those followers, whose lives were dramatically shortened by malnutrition and lack of faith in modern medicine, would have been better off eschewing silly superstitions and occult mysticism for a normal life outside the walls of the Cloister.

15.
PORTRAIT OF AN EXECUTIONER
(CENTRE COUNTY)

On a crisp October day in 1939, a thin man in wire-rim spectacles left his mother's house on Ellis Avenue in Pittsburgh and traveled across the Allegheny Plateau to his new job in Centre County. Quiet and soft-spoken with a receding hairline, 37-year-old Frank Lee Wilson looked like the nondescript, timid sort of man whose job might be that of an accountant or perhaps a high school science teacher. In fact, once upon a time, Frank Lee Wilson did teach electrical engineering classes at a local vocational school, but his new workplace was a far cry from the classrooms of South High School. His new employer was Rockview Prison in Bellefonte, which, at the time, was a branch of the Western Penitentiary. His talents as an electrician would prove indispensable in his new role as the first official executioner for the Commonwealth of Pennsylvania.

The rise and fall of Frank Lee Wilson is a remarkable tale; it is the tragic story of a quiet, tiny man tasked with the awesome responsibility of meting out justice to the state's most hardened and repugnant criminals. It is a cautionary tale about how a mild-mannered individual can turn into a cruel, hardened shell of a human being in just a few short years after being granted the God-like power of revoking human life.

THE WARDEN AND MR. X

It was July of 1938 when Warden Stanley P. Ashe offered Wilson the position as Mr. X, which, for the sake of anonymity, had long been the unofficial name of the man who flipped the switch of Old Sparky, the state's infamous electric chair. Although Wilson would become the state's first full-time executioner, several different men had filled the role of Mr. X since the first convict was executed by electrocution in Pennsylvania in 1915. In those days, executioners traveled from state to state plying their grisly trade, and the man Wilson was replacing, Robert Elliott, was a legend in the annals of capital punishment.

Elliott, who expertly executed 387 prisoners in Pennsylvania and neighboring states during his career—more than any other American executioner—had been mulling over retirement for quite a while due to health reasons but continued to perform his job until Warden Ashe was able to find a suitable replacement. Frank Lee Wilson had attracted the warden's attention while supervising the installation of a new lighting system at Pittsburgh's Western Penitentiary. The project took two years to complete, and during this time Wilson and the warden had developed a close friendship.

Wilson, however, was hesitant to accept the position as Robert Elliott's successor. Perhaps he was aware of the jinx that plagued Pennsylvania's previous executioners; this first man to pull the switch at Rockview was Maurice Broderick, who racked up 166 executions before being crushed to death by a crane at the age of 37 while supervising a prison construction project in 1926. There was Sylvester McNeal, one of the early traveling executioners, who died of a heart attack in the warden's office after performing an electrocution in Ohio, and John Hulbert, who shot himself in the head in 1926. There was Edward Davis, who grew so disgusted by his work that he quit abruptly one day and lived the rest of his life in solitude as a hermit. Of the amateur Rockview executioner who electrocuted wife slayer Mike Louisa in 1916, not much is known other than the fact that he was an engineering student at Penn State University who was called upon to "pinch hit" for Maurice Broderick.

Even the legendary Robert Elliott had seen his house blown up in 1928 after he pulled the switch on anarchists Nicola Sacco and Bartolomeo Vanzetti at Charlestown State Prison in Massachusetts, which required a police booth to be erected in his yard with an officer assigned to guard him until the day of his death. It was around this time he suffered a nervous breakdown after pulling the switch on a female prisoner, and friends and colleagues observed that he was never the same man ever again. Shortly before his death on October 10, 1939, Elliott became an outspoken critic of the electric chair. "It doesn't do any good," he said repeatedly. "There is a certain satisfaction the state gets, a sort of revenge. But we keep on getting these terrible criminals just the same." It is understandable why Frank Lee Wilson needed some time to make up his mind.

Nevertheless, Wilson accepted the position, which paid $250 per electrocution and $100 for any additional execution performed on the same day. As part of the agreement, Wilson was permitted to keep his regular job at the Raphael Electric Construction Company. On the night of October 23, 1939, he arrived at Rockview neatly-dressed in an Oxford gray pinstripe suit, white shirt, and blue and white tie. He would return home to his mother, wife and two children the next day $450 richer.

FROM DUCK HUNTER TO OVERNIGHT CELEBRITY

Wilson did not have the luxury of easing into his new role. Just as soon as he was hired, he was called upon to perform a triple execution, and the rookie executioner took his place behind the switch at 12:31 and calmly and coolly dispatched his victims in under fifteen minutes. The first prisoner that day was Paul Ferry, who had slaughtered his wife three years earlier with an axe inside their Erie home. With three flips of a switch, Wilson sent 2,000 volts of electricity into Ferry's body, but it was evident that Wilson lacked the finesse of his predecessor. According to reports, Wilson applied the first jolt ten seconds longer than was the custom, which caused "smoke to mushroom from the prisoner's head" and the body to break out in blisters—Ferry had been cooked well beyond the 240-degree electrocution temperature. However, Wilson refined his technique and flawlessly electrocuted Willie Bailey and Ira Redmon by 12:46.

After the task was complete, Wilson lit a cigarette and chatted with Warden Ashe, who invited Wilson to his home for dinner that night, where he introduced the new Mr. X to reporters. Ashe heaped praise upon Wilson, telling the press, "He recognizes the law as it is. He is a public servant and feels no more responsible for an electrocution than the judge and the jury." Although Wilson appeared reticent to talk to reporters, the bespectacled electrician virtually became an overnight celebrity.

Upon returning home, Wilson grabbed his shotgun and headed to Pymatuning Dam. Hunting was his passion, and when he returned from his trip, he was met by a throng of newspaper reporters.

"Come in, fellows, I was just stuffing a duck," said Wilson to his visitors. But if they had been expecting the same timid man they had met at the warden's home a few days earlier, they were in for a pleasant surprise. Wilson seemed to revel in his newfound celebrity and talked freely about his job, and his philosophy pertaining to capital punishment. "These fellows may come from good families, and it's just too bad that they get in jams, but the job has to be done," Wilson said to reporters from the Pittsburgh *Sun-Telegraph* and insisted that the electric chair was the most humane method of imposing the death sentence.

"What the general public doesn't realize is that a person is rendered unconscious by the first shock," he explained. "After that, death comes quickly and is painless. The victims don't suffer."

A COOL AND METHODICAL KILLER

Because of Wilson's sudden fame as the state's first full-time executioner, the public clamored for more information about the bookish electrician's personal life. For most citizens, this was the first time they had ever been able to connect a name with the mysterious death-dealer known previously only as Mr. X. They found every detail about his home and work life fascinating, from his living arrangement taking care of his elderly mother at her North Side home to his parenting of two young boys, Robert and Frankie. The public seemed especially fond of the new executioner after it was reported that he had learned his trade by taking night classes at the Carnegie Institute of Technology while working a day job to support his family. He quickly rose through the ranks of electricians and worked in New York for several years as a supervisor in an engineering firm. State officials described Wilson as "a poor, deserving electrician" who was selected for the job at Rockview after Warden Ashe had been dissatisfied with the seventy applications he had received for the position of Mr. X.

The public also followed the executions at Rockview Penitentiary closely. After Wilson experienced a little trouble dispatching armed robbers Charles Golden and Walter Tankard to their maker on October 30, the Pittsburgh *Press* remarked that the prison physician, Dr. Schwartz, slowly shook his head after listening to the heart of Golden. Wilson calmly reapplied the current and gave the condemned man a second shock and, finally, a third. Wilson also required three contacts to execute Tankard, causing the *Press* reporter to lament that this was "something that has not happened within the memory of veteran observers," many of whom noted that Robert Elliott could've done the job with only one contact apiece. Nevertheless, observers also noted that Wilson appeared "cool and methodical," operating the switch with one hand while glancing at his watch on the other. This was to become his trademark style.

While Frank Lee Wilson was a hero to some, others viewed him as a villain—a state-sanctioned killer who, if history were any indication, would someday crack under the strain of his gruesome job. Dark family secrets began to spill out, such as the fact that his older brother, Walter Boyd, had been arrested in 1924 on a felony count of smuggling whiskey and other contraband into prison for Western Penitentiary inmates while working at the facility as a guard, resulting in a drunken riot in which two of his fellow guards were slain. Little is known of the mother of his children, but census records show that she was not living at the Wilson home on Ellis Avenue.

A MYSTERIOUS MARRIAGE

But there was love in the air for Mr. X; on June 21, 1941, Wilson married 35-year-old Caroline Knueppe of Pittsburgh in a secret ceremony in the West Virginia panhandle. There's some mystery involved in this union; the application for the marriage license was filed in Brooke County, but the minister's return of endorsement clearly shows the document was signed by Alfred Martin of Chester, West Virginia, which happens to be in neighboring Hancock County. Strangely, Martin had crossed out the term "minister of the Gospel," which was pre-printed on the marriage record. In other words, it is unclear whether Frank and Caroline were married in Hancock or Brooke County and whether or not Alfred Martin was really an ordained minister; there appears to be no other mention of him in

Chester church records (and Chester is a small town), and every other minister who completed marriage applications in Brooke County signed their names with the title of Reverend.

The following year, Wilson was approached by a warden from South Dakota to assist him in designing that state's first electric chair, but wartime shortages of copper wire forced Wilson to scrap his planned trip to Sioux Falls. After the death of his mother, he relocated with his wife to a modest brick house at 160 Crestview Drive in the Pleasant Hill neighborhood of Pittsburgh, where he continued to work by day as an electrical engineer.

There was no shortage of work for Wilson at Rockview, however; Mr. X pulled the switch on dozens of killers over the next few years, which included the likes of John Childers, Michael Musto, Herbert Green, "Big Mike" Bubna, Shellie McKeathen, Frederick Morris, William Kenny Wilson (who had the uncanny fate of being sentenced to death by a judge named Wilson and electrocuted by a man named Wilson), William Ramage, Grant Holley, Rufus Keller, and Corrine Sykes, who was the first female in fifteen years to die in Rockview's electric chair.

SCANDAL ROCKS ROCKVIEW

By this time, death row inmates and prison officials weren't the only ones who had come to regard Frank Lee Wilson as impassively cool and emotionless. Citing "cruel and barbarous treatment" at the hands of her husband, Caroline Wilson walked out of their Pleasant Hills home in the summer of 1951 and promptly hired an attorney, Charles W. Herald, and sued for a "bed and board" separation. Unlike a divorce, this arrangement would prevent either party from legally remarrying and could result in the family property and assets being divided equally if a judge saw fit. Frank Wilson called his wife's accusations "bunkum" and immediately gave his side of the story to the press.

According to Frank, on the night of August 16, the Wilsons had finished watching television, and Frank had gone to bed when Caroline, upset over some trivial matter, began slamming doors and rattling the blinds in a fashion not in keeping with the lateness of the hour. He ordered her to "cut out the three-ring circus" and come to bed. He admitted that he may have shoved her toward the bed. Caroline went to a neighbor's house and contacted a justice of the peace. In the morning, Frank left for a fishing trip on the Chesapeake Bay and returned five days later. During this time, Mrs. Wilson had gone to St. Francis Hospital for an examination, but doctors told Frank they had x-rayed Caroline but failed to find any sign of injury. Frank pointed out that he had been the one who had called the authorities on his wife two years earlier after she had threatened him with a gun, warning him, "I can shoot as straight as you." After this first separation, they had agreed to divide $7000 in savings bonds between themselves. "I hope she comes back," Frank added, but Caroline was unmoved. She took up residence at an apartment complex on Baywood Street in Mt. Lebanon.

The real-life soap opera would play itself out in local papers until its ugly and controversial conclusion in 1953. By this time, Warden Ashe had stepped down from the helm of Western Penitentiary and Rockview and was replaced by the long-time superintendent, Dr. John W. Claudy, who was also a close personal friend of Wilson. After a series of bloody riots rocked both facilities on January 18 of that year, Governor John S. Fine empaneled a commission spearheaded by Jacob L. Devers to investigate the matter. The scathing report of the Devers Committee sent shockwaves across Pennsylvania, with its accusations of unsanitary conditions, rampant "sex perversion," inhumane treatment of prisoners, and its declaration that sweeping changes needed to be made all the way from the top down to the "least custodial officer." The Devers report also blamed guards for allowing liquor, weapons and other contraband to be smuggled into both facilities. Surely, these findings must've weighed heavily upon the executioner, whose brother had been charged with the same crimes three decades earlier.

Claudy, an ordained Presbyterian minister who had previously served as prison chaplain, fired back with a seventeen-page retort of his own before resigning on May 2, against the advice of the prison's board of trustees. He was immediately joined by Frank Lee Wilson, who was said to have remarked, "If Claudy goes, so do I." He told reporters that both he and Claudy had been contemplating retirement long before the January 18 riots and that the findings of the Devers Committee had nothing at all to do with his decision. Wilson was credited with 55 executions at the time of his resignation. "I started to resign three years ago," said Wilson, "but Dr. Claudy was carrying a heavy load. I promised I wouldn't let him down but that I would leave when he did." The heavy load to which he was referring was the death of Claudy's granddaughter following an operation, and the disgraced warden verified this statement.

"My plans to retire are merely coincidental with the present situation," Claudy told reporters. "They have been in the making for some time, prior to any disturbance or investigation at the institution. My retirement is hastened by a personal tragedy in my own family." A few days later, deputy warden William Gaffney resigned from his post of twenty years.

A RUINED MAN

The fallout from the damning Devers report led to the separation of Western Penitentiary from Rockview in 1953, which, up to that time, had been a "branch" of the Pittsburgh institution. As for Mr. X, he was unscathed by the scandal—his estranged wife had already destroyed his reputation.

The legal proceedings between Frank and Caroline reached a new level of bitterness just days after the prison riots, months before the findings of the Devers Committee had been made public. On January 29, 1953, she testified before Judge Homer S. Brown that she had received no financial support from her husband since their separation two years earlier. She then told Judge Brown that the troubles began soon after their marriage in West Virginia. She claimed that Frank had given her a black eye during an altercation in 1943 and offered a photograph of her injury as proof, and claimed that a few years later, things turned physical during a game of bridge.

"He threw his cards in the fireplace," Caroline stated. "As I got up, he hit me and knocked me the length of the room." Caroline Wilson then told the judge about an altercation in July of 1948, in which Frank knocked out one of her front teeth after she had accidentally stepped on his glasses. "I bear a scar under my nose to this day," she said. Other incidents, according to Mrs. Wilson, included her husband threatening to break her neck and attempting to run her over with his car. But her most startling accusation was that her husband had once beaten her so badly that it left her face partially paralyzed for six months. It's anyone's guess whether or not Caroline had a flair for melodrama or exaggeration, but Frank didn't seem to have much of an interest in defending his reputation. Instead, he quietly reached a settlement whereby he agreed to pay his estranged wife $145 a month in support.

Jerry Kraemer assumed the position of state executioner in 1954, though Wilson was present at a handful of Kraemer's first executions to offer advice. Much like Robert Elliott, Kraemer's opinion of capital punishment eventually changed, and he resigned his position after pulling the switch nineteen times in his eight years on the job.

The last days of Frank Lee Wilson are shrouded in mystery, with some newspaper articles claiming that he became an alcoholic and died impoverished in the county poorhouse a few years later. He never remarried, and neither did Caroline, who passed away on July 11, 1966.

16.

THE BLACK PHANTOM OF THE SCOTIA BARRENS

(CENTRE COUNTY)

"I don't know what made me do it. I just grabbed her by the head with one hand and threw her down, and with the other hand, I cut her throat." This was the explication given by Bert Delige in 1910 after he had senselessly slaughtered Mrs. John Baudis of Scotia, a once-thriving Centre County mining town just west of State College. Today, Scotia is a ghost town—and one of the strangest ghost towns in a state filled that is filled with them, because, unlike other Pennsylvania ghost towns, this one actually has a ghost.

As for a motive, Delige gave none; Hulda Baudis had simply been walking home from her sister's house when she was accosted in a cornfield, and her throat was slashed with a razor blade. The killer carried out the crime just as calmly and mindlessly as one goes about brushing their teeth or taking out the trash. Perhaps there was just something strange in the air that fateful day in 1910, although anyone who has ever visited the infamous Scotia Barrens is likely to tell you that there is always something strange in the air.

Of course, some will say that the perpetual chill is due to a natural phenomenon caused by the trapping of air currents blown down from the mountains, creating what climatologists call a "frost pocket." Geologists might say the sparseness of vegetation around the Barrens is caused by the excessively sandy, acidic soil, which contains little organic matter. But those who have encountered the ghost of Black Bert roaming the Barrens might have a different explanation, for the Barrens have always been a dead zone in more ways than one—a place where tragedy grew just a little bit taller than the scrawny and stunted trees fringing the fruitless landscape.

THE FOUNDING OF SCOTIA

Scotia owes its existence to steel magnate Andrew Carnegie, who held the leases to several ore-bearing tracts of land in Patton Township in the late 19th century. Although iron mining in the region had been carried out on a small scale since the Revolutionary War, it was Carnegie who, in 1880, dreamed of exploiting Centre County's natural resources to the fullest extent. Carnegie, who was a Scottish immigrant, named the place as a tribute to his homeland, and his men soon began mining iron ore from a large, open pit. After washing the ore to separate it from clay, the men loaded it onto railroad cars bound for the steel mills of Pittsburgh. Unfortunately for Carnegie, the venture didn't turn out to be the financial success he had envisioned. In 1899, Carnegie sold the land to the Bellefonte Furnace Company, which operated the Scotia ore fields until 1911, when the mine was closed and the village was abandoned.

Like most Pennsylvania ghost towns, Scotia popped up virtually overnight and seemed to disappear just as quickly. Today, all that remains are abandoned concrete ghosts of Scotia's failed resurrection in the 1940s, when the mine was briefly re-opened. These remnants include parts of an ore washery and bits and pieces of the Graysdale-Scotia spur of the Bellefonte Central Railroad. During its heyday in the late 19th century, however, Scotia boasted a population of around four hundred, and the village contained a church, school, saloon, a handful of shops and a public library. The town band, known as the Forest Cornet Band, would often strike up a tune whenever the village's founder, Andrew Carnegie, decided to pay a visit (which, by all accounts, was a regular occurrence).

THE DARK SIDE OF SCOTIA

While Scotia is known as the home of convicted murderer Bert Delige, "Black Bert" wasn't the first killer to inhabit the Barrens. Simon Dunshot was a German immigrant who arrived in the Barrens sometime in the 1880s and found employment as an ore washer. While returning to Germany for a visit in 1893, Dunshot was arrested as an anarchist and thrown into prison. He escaped by blowing up the jail (and an adjoining building or two) with dynamite, snuffing out a few lives in the process. After his escape, he made his way to Minnesota before returning to Patton Township, where he was eventually tracked down by a detective, C.F. Alexander, and an attorney working on behalf of the German government named Carl Hartman. Dunshot was arrested in Scotia in July of 1895, but not before putting up a whale of a fight. The Altoona *Tribune* reported that while Dunshot was tussling with the detective, the fugitive's twelve-year-old son attacked Hartman with a knife. Fortunately for Hartman, the assault didn't amount to very much; the paper also reported that the lawyer "succeeded in wrenching the knife from the boy's hands and put it in his pocket... He will keep it as a memento of an exciting experience outside his usual business." As for Dunshot, he was last seen being chained to a seat on a train bound for New York. He was extradited to Germany and summarily executed for his activities.

While authorities in Germany were dispensing with Dunshot, a quiet funeral was taking place in West Scotia, which was then known as Marysville. Aaron Delige, a Civil War veteran (who served in the same company as Siege of Petersburg hero and Medal of Honor recipient Franklin Hogan), was being laid to rest in the Marysville African Methodist Episcopal Cemetery. Delige would have the honor of being the last burial in the churchyard. In a few short years, the Delige family name would come to be tarnished thanks to the Civil War veteran's grandson.

Bert Delige, Aaron's grandson, was the son of John and Christina Delige. John had frequent run-ins with the law, often for gambling, fighting, and the keeping of innumerable "disorderly houses" between Bellefonte and Tyrone. Although his date of death is unclear, it appears that John was long gone from Bert's life before the murder of Mrs. Baudis in Scotia. In February of 1925, Bert's brother, Walter, was struck over the head with a stove shaker by a cousin, Herbert Kreitz (whose father was married to Jane Delige), who fled the scene and whose body was later found along the banks of Spring Creek with four bullet wounds in the chest and one in the head. Because a revolver was found in Kreitz's hand, the death was ruled a suicide, although one has to wonder how a person could inflict five potentially fatal gunshot wounds to one's head and chest and still manage to hold on to the suicide weapon.

Not all of the Centre County Deliges were lawless; however, some just happened to marry spouses who were. Sadie Delige, of Bellefonte, was a star trapeze performer for the Barnum & Bailey Circus many years before her death in 1923 (at least according to her obituary). Sadie's first husband, Jacob Dean, famously burnt to a crisp in a Bedford County jail cell in 1881 after setting fire to his mattress while in an intoxicated state. Because virtually every Delige family death certificate from Centre County is filled out with "not known" under the name of the decedent's father, date of birth, and maiden name of mother, it's hard to say exactly how the Deliges are related to each other, but it's clear that the Delige-Kreitz family tree extended to Clearfield County, Blair County, and Cattaraugus County, New York.

As for Bert Delige, who lived with his mother and six siblings on his grandfather's 18-acre farm in Scotia, little is known about his life prior to 1905, when he returned home after a stint at the Huntingdon Reformatory. Soon after his return from reform school (he apparently had attempted to rob a Scotia grocer at gunpoint), he shot and killed a child named Ralph Williams in the village schoolyard.

On the afternoon of October 20, Delige was heading into the woods with his shotgun to do some hunting when 13-year-old Ralph Williams stopped him. "Wait a minute, I want to tell you something," said Williams, running up to Delige. It was reported that Delige pointed the gun at the youth "in a spirit of playfulness" and pulled the trigger, not knowing the weapon was loaded. The blast tore off Williams' calf, resulting in a serious loss of blood. Williams was carried to the home of a local physician, who advised the boy's father to take him to the Altoona Hospital at once. Ralph was placed on the main line express train but passed away in his father's arms before the train reached its destination. When the train stopped at the Bellwood station, Mr. Williams telephoned the Centre County sheriff, who arrested Bert Delige without incident. Delige was tried the following month and convicted of murder in the second degree. In May of 1906, he was sentenced to a three-year term at the Western Penitentiary.

DEATH OF THE MERRY-GO-ROUND MAN

Known as the "Merry-Go-Round Man," John Baudis made his living operating carousels at fairs and carnivals around central Pennsylvania. Bert Delige had worked for Baudis at one time but had abandoned his employment after a dispute over unpaid wages. On August 15, 1910, John Baudis met his death under unusual circumstances; while operating a merry-go-round at a fireman's carnival in South Williamsport, Baudis became angry and went into his tent, where he blew out his brains with a revolver. Although he had penned a suicide note to his wife before taking his own life, Baudis never revealed the cause of his troubles. Hulda Baudis traveled to Lycoming County by train to retrieve the body of her husband, unaware that she would shortly be reunited with him on the other side of the grave.

While the murder of Hulda Baudis and the subsequent execution of Bert Delige have been written about extensively in books on Centre County, it's safe to say that a great deal of what has been written has been exaggerated for the sake of storytelling. For instance, in James Frazier's otherwise excellent book, *The Black Ghost of Scotia and More Pennsylvania Fireside Tales*, the author cites Tom McKivison of Bellefonte, who reminisced about the murder in 1985. According to McKivison, the night of the murder—October 16, 1910—was an unusually clear and bright moonlit evening. However, astronomical records show that the moon had not even reached its first quarter stage on the night of the murder. In reality, it was a very dark and dreary night.

Rather than relying upon the 75-year-old recollections of old-timers, perhaps it is better to rely upon the words of the killer himself. Shortly after his conviction, Bert Delige gave a full confession to a Bellefonte newspaper reporter and talked about his life and the crime that brought him statewide notoriety. Delige stated:

"There isn't much that I can tell about myself. I am twenty-eight years old and was born up at Scotia. When I was a youngster I ran about the mines up there and played with the other boys. I went to school after a while. I can't just tell how old I was just then, but I guess I went to school about four months.

"The first work I ever did was when I was eight or ten years old . . . I can remember all about it even now. I started out to work on the farm of Samuel T. Gray, and he sent me up to Gray's cemetery to whitewash the pailings. The next work I did, as near as I can tell, was to pick potatoes on the Gray farm." Delige then worked a succession of jobs ranging from carrying slate and lead to working in a brickyard. At one time, he also worked in the Scotia ore washery, but his fate was sealed the day he decided to go to work for John and Hulda Baudis.

"The first time I ever worked for Mr. Baudis was when he started out with his merry-go-round," stated Delige. "I don't know what year that was. I was working at Philipsburg then. Mr. Baudis had his merry-go-round down at Hecla. One night, his son (Edward Baudis) was coming in from Osceola. He got off the train at Philipsburg and didn't get back on in time and, in that way, missed his train. He didn't have any money and came to me where I was shantying and asked me if there was any way he could get to Hecla."

According to Delige, he suggested hopping a freight train. He and Edward Baudis hopped on a freight train to Tyrone, and from there, they went to Hecla by passenger train, with Delige footing the bill. The young men never saw each other after that, so Delige attempted to get the money he was owed from Mr. and Mrs. Baudis, but to no avail. Basically, Bert Delige slit the throat of Hulda Baudis over train fare.

In his confession, Delige admitted to hiding in the bushes and lying in wait for his victim on her return from visiting neighbors. He leaped upon Hulda Baudis as she passed, dragged her into the bushes and raped her. He left his victim unconscious along the roadside but returned to the scene because he had apparently forgotten his hat. By the time he returned, Mrs. Baudis was just regaining consciousness, and she recognized her assailant. Fearing that she would scream for help, Delige produced a razor and slit her throat from ear to ear.

THE TRIAL AND EXECUTION OF BERT DELIGE

When the body of Mrs. Baudis was discovered on the morning of October 17 in a cornfield by the earthen dam at the Scotia reservoir, it was at first assumed that she had killed herself while in a state of despair over the death of her husband. But when authorities failed to find a knife or razor at the scene, it became clear that Mrs. Baudis had been murdered. Not surprisingly, Delige was the leading suspect from the start.

Delige was arrested and arraigned on November 10, 1910. During his preliminary hearing, an expert testified that the clothing worn by Delige on the night of the murder was splotched with blood, and evidence was offered to show that Mrs. Baudis' death was caused by either a knife or razor. But although no murder weapon had been recovered, Delige was bound over for trial without bail, presumably in light of his confession. However, about two weeks later, detectives discovered a razor belonging to the accused hidden beneath a tree stump on his family's property. This discovery of this key piece of evidence is what would ultimately lead Bert Delige to the gallows and earn him the distinction of being the last man executed in Centre County by hanging.

On December 10, Delige was found guilty of murder in the first degree and sentenced to death. Sheriff Hurley announced that no passes would be issued to visitors seeking admittance to the execution, which was to be held inside the Centre County jail yard in Bellefonte on April 25, 1911.

Despite the sensational nature of the crime, the execution was carried out with little fanfare. No members of the Delige family were present, and only one son of Mrs. Baudis was on hand to witness the hanging. On the morning of his last day on earth, Delige ate a hearty breakfast and went to the scaffold without fear or emotion, accompanied by Reverend P.F. Paul, Rev. H.N. Hepler, Sheriff Hurley and Deputy Sheriff Rees. At the scaffold Delige gave a three-minute speech urging all to live upright lives. His last words were, "I have only a few minutes to live, but I'll soon be in the arms of Jesus. I'm not afraid." The trap was sprung at 10:17 a.m., and Delige was pronounced dead 14 minutes and 39 seconds later.

Because of the ghastly nature of his crime, the body of Bert Delige was not permitted to be buried in the West Scotia (Marysville) cemetery and was interred on his family property in a grave marked by a flat, uncarved stone. Since the cemetery property adjoined the Delige property, the murderer's grave lies within about fifty yards of the cemetery boundary, near the spot where the family home once stood.

According to Scotia native Tom McKivison, who was eight years of age when the murder took place, there was no ceremony prior to the burial. "I was standing right there when they did it, looking over the wire fence," McKivison told the Centre *Daily Times* in 1985. "There wasn't any service. They just put him in the ground and marked the grave with a flat stone." McKivison recalled that he and his wife returned to visit Scotia for several years. "The last time we went, I could still find the place they buried Bert, but that flat stone wasn't there no more. Somebody took it, I guess. Don't know why."

THE GHOST OF BLACK BERT

Perhaps it was this act of vandalism that lured Bert Delige's spirit from the realm of the dead because that appears to be around the time stories of a black supernatural entity prowling the Barrens began to circulate. The first documented sighting comes from 1977 when a Centre County historian named Hugh Winchester was doing research in a local library. He overheard a conversation between a library staffer and an unfamiliar man, who claimed that he had been out with some friends at the Barrens one night when they saw a "large black figure" moving toward them. The gigantic apparition seemed to float through the air, and the men observed this ghostly figure for several minutes before it disappeared. Manchester, who was aware of the story of Bert Delige, asked the man where exactly this sighting occurred, and he recognized it as the exact spot where Mrs. Baudis had been murdered. He also asked the man the date of the sighting, and sure enough, it was April 25—the day Delige was executed. Since that time, there have been scores of reported sightings of the "Black Ghost of the Barrens" from hunters, hikers, and others who have roamed the Scotia wilderness.

17.
THE TRAGIC HISTORY OF DEADMAN CORNERS
(FOREST COUNTY)

Amid the sprawling wilderness of the Allegheny National Forest, miles from the nearest town, four roads converge in a remote spot in Howe Township, where a wooden cross marks the lonesome grave of a murder victim long forgotten. Although the name 'Turner' is etched into the weather-beaten memorial, most locals can't quite say who the unfortunate man was or when he died; all they can tell you is that it happened long, long ago.

This simple burial plot at the junction of Job Corps Road, Coal Bed Run Road, Blood Run Road and Deadman Corners Road is known locally by a variety of names, but the one that seems to have stuck is Peddler's Grave because legend has it that the victim in question was a traveling peddler who was robbed, murdered, then buried on the spot where his body was discovered. But the historical record makes it clear that this wilderness gravesite in Forest County is the final resting place of a woodsman named Matthew Turner, who was murdered on this very spot on September 9, 1871, by William Barnhart.

Matthew Turner was a broad-shouldered, good-natured, red-haired woodsman of about fifty years of age who lived on the farm of Thomas

Porter, which was located on the road between Marienville and Balltown (which once stood along Tionesta Creek at a point opposite Logan Run). At the time, Balltown was scarcely more than a few shacks that had sprung up around the lumber mill Isaac Ball had built in 1823. On the morning of Saturday, September 9, Turner left the Porter farm to go to his shanty in the lumber camp on Foxburg Road, where he worked (Foxburg was located on Tionesta Creek, at a point opposite Bluejay Creek). Turner never made it to camp, but his absence drew little attention. Lumber camps were filled with vagabonds, ruffians, ex-convicts and drifters who seldom stuck around past their first payday, so it was probably assumed that Turner had found employment elsewhere.

Neither hide nor hair was seen of Turner until Wednesday when Thomas Porter returned home from a business trip to Marienville and decided to pay a visit to Turner's shanty. Not finding his friend at the Foxburg lumber camp, Porter followed the route Matthew Turner should have taken. He discovered Turner's body lying on the side of the road about two miles from the shanty. A hasty examination revealed to Porter that his friend had been shot in the head and neck. He summoned the authorities and an inquest was held at the scene of the crime.

It was discovered that Turner's head and neck were filled with buckshot, and the position of the body seemed to suggest that his assassin had lain in wait for him before ambushing the victim from behind. Death must have been instantaneous, and Turner went to his death never knowing the identity of his killer. Turner's rifle was found leaning against a log, and his hatchet was found nearby, indicating that Turner had sat down on the log to rest when the fatal shot was fired. He had a knife and revolver in his belt, neither of which had been disturbed. Because his body was already in an advanced state of decomposition, it was buried on the spot where it had been found.

The inquest failed to shed any light on the identity of the killer, but many suspected that the murderer had been William Barnhart, a notorious troublemaker who had terrorized the vicinity for quite some time. Barnhart was known to be crazy and, for some reason, harbored a deep hatred toward anyone with red hair—man, woman or child. As fate would have it, Turner was red-headed. A search was made for Barnhart, but his unexplained absence from his usual haunts aroused the suspicion of local lawmen Henry Bailey and James K. Clark, who eventually tracked him to Jefferson County and brought him to Tionesta, where he was bound over for trial without bail.

FOREST COUNTY'S FIRST MURDER TRIAL

The first murder trial in the history of Forest County began on December 28, 1871, with Judge Wetmore presiding. The attorneys for the Commonwealth were District Attorney W.W. Mason, W.P. Mercilliott, and ex-judge S.P. Johnson. Samuel D. Irwin and B.J. Reed defended William Barnhart. Although there were no witnesses to the crime and the evidence was circumstantial at best, it took the jury only a few minutes to find the defendant not guilty by reason of insanity. The jury's verdict, which was printed in the Tionesta *Forest Republican* on January 9, 1872, read:

We find that the defendant, William Barnhart, was insane at the time he committed the offense for which he is indicted and acquit him on the grounds of such insanity. The Jury also, on full examination, find that there is reason to believe a cure of such insanity may speedily be effected by sending said William Barnhart to the Lunatic Hospital. Whereupon the Court direct the defendant to be committed to the Insane Hospital at Dixmont for so long a time as he shall continue to be of unsound mind, at the expense of the County of Forest.

During the trial, Barnhart's hatred of red-headed people was revealed by an entry in the killer's diary, in which Barnhart wrote that they should all be killed. Barnhart's mother and one of his sisters testified on his behalf and said that William had never acted strangely until his return from the army. Perhaps he had been shot at by a red-headed Confederate soldier, or perhaps his heart had been broken by a red-haired Southern belle, but Barnhart never revealed the cause of his intense prejudice.

William Barnhart was committed to the Dixmont Insane Asylum, where he attempted to kill a red-headed guard, but was transferred to the Warren State Hospital upon its opening in 1880. Barnhart was never "cured" of his insanity, and he died at Warren State Hospital on March 10, 1911, at the age of 70, and is buried at the state hospital cemetery.

18.
THE VEILED LADY OF PENN PARK
(YORK COUNTY)

In 1903, the residents of the city of York were terrorized by the appearance of a woman in a long black veil who strolled through Penn Park every night, imploring frightened passersby to lift her veil and take a peek. As if this nightly occurrence wasn't bizarre enough, it just so happened that Penn Park was once the site of a potter's field where York's impoverished and unknown dead had been buried in unmarked graves, as well as the site of a Civil War hospital.

HISTORY OF THE COMMONS
When the city of York was laid out in 1741, tracts of land were reserved on both sides of Codorus Creek for public use. To the early residents of the city, these tracts were known as "The Commons" and were originally utilized as pasture for cattle and sheep. After the tract west of Codorus Creek was sold, the commons east of the creek, which totaled 20 acres, became the property of the Commonwealth. In 1816 these public lands were deeded to the city of York and renamed the Public Common. This deed also conveyed to the city two lots to be used as a potter's field, "to be kept as a public burial place forever, and for no other use, intent or purpose."

These twenty acres have a long and colorful history; during the Colonial Era, when the Continental Congress held its sessions in York, an entire regiment of soldiers encamped at the Commons. In the fall of 1814, during our second war with the British, over 7,000 soldiers made their camp at the site in anticipation of an attack after the British burned Washington. In the following years, when all young and able-bodied citizens were required by law to participate in militia training, the Commons were used four times a year for drills and exercises.

In 1842, six acres of the Commons fronting South George Street were sold, and the remaining 14 acres were put to use as circus and exhibition grounds; the first York County fair was held on this spot in October of 1853. Barracks for the Sixth New York Cavalry were erected on the Public Commons in 1861 for use as winter quarters. From 1862 to 1865, the northern portion of the Commons was used as a military hospital. During the Battle of Gettysburg, over 14,000 sick and wounded Union soldiers were cared for by nurses and surgeons at this hospital.

After the war, the Commons became a neglected and overgrown spot. Locals used the southern portion as a garbage dump, and this spot was the home of "Squire" Braxton, a freed slave from Virginia who built himself a shack out of discarded junk. Squire Braxton (whose real name was Charles Granger), along with his dozen dogs, remained the sole occupant of the Public Commons until his death.

POTTER'S FIELD AND THE CREATION OF PENN PARK

In 1890, local businessman A.B. Farquhar contributed $1,400 toward the construction of a public park. Trees were planted, walkways were laid out, and the Commons were cleaned up. In 1898, the mayor appointed a Board of Park Commissioners, and Penn Park was dedicated with an impressive ceremony on June 15, 1898. At the park's center, a monument to the York County soldiers of the Civil War was erected at a cost of $25,000.

However, while the park soon became a place for joyful picnics and band concerts, grim darkness lurked at its borders. On April 28, 1897, by order of the Court of Common Pleas, the potter's field at the northern section of the Public Commons was sold to the York City School Board for the erection of a new school (William Penn High School now occupies this spot). Under this agreement, the school board was responsible for the excavation and removal of bodies to the new potter's field, which had been established on the York and Harrisburg Turnpike. This, of course, violated the original 1816 deed, which guaranteed that the potter's field would be used as "a public burial ground forever" and that said land could not be used for a different purpose.

Even before the sale was finalized, the school board sought ways to cut costs. They agreed that the excavation would be limited to the immediate site of the proposed school building only, an area 80 by 155 feet in dimension. Because of a boundary disagreement between the school board and the English Catholic Church (now St. Patrick's Church), which stands across the potter's field on South Beaver Street, the portion of the grounds used by the church for its stable was not excavated. Records show that the York School District spent $461.94 on dynamite and disinfectant during the hasty removal of bodies that had reposed in peace since 1816.

Although the Board of Health estimated that 600 bodies were buried at Potter's Field, work was suspended after just 168 bodies had been excavated by order of President Evans of the school board, after an investigation showed that the school board had been misspending funds. The reason for the cost-cutting measures was that the excavation operation had been horribly mismanaged up to that point, with the school board purchasing hemlock coffins for $1.25 apiece while less-expensive coffins were locally available for just fifty cents each. It was also revealed that, out of the 161 workers hired for the project, twelve had gotten their jobs through local political connections. Even worse, these unscrupulous workers had exhausted taxpayer funds by falsifying their time cards and claiming wages for work they did not perform. This financial scandal caused the York *Dispatch*, on April 19, 1897, to hail the scandal as "one of the most notorious pieces of political jobbery ever perpetrated in York."

Work resumed in late April, and by month's end, 323 of the approximate 600 bodies had been excavated and reburied. The total number of bodies excavated from the old Public Commons is unclear, but for years afterward, ghost stories abounded in the vicinity of Penn Park amid rumors that an untold number of bodies had been left behind in the school board's haste and scandal-inspired cost-cutting measures. When the new high school opened in September of 1899, six thousand children marched in a parade from Centre Square and across Penn Park to the new school for the dedication ceremonies, perhaps unknowingly trampling on the bones of the long-forgotten dead.

THE VEILED LADY

With its history as a military hospital and burial grounds, it is not surprising that Penn Park soon became the topic of ghost stories and strange tales, though none are as strange as the story of the Veiled Lady, who made her appearance in the fall of 1903.

In early October, residents walking through the park after dark reported the presence of a woman dressed in black, her face covered by a veil, who approached them at random and implored them to lift her veil. On the night of Wednesday, October 7, the veiled woman approached a young man and asked him for the time. After giving her the time, the mysterious woman asked, "Don't you recognize me?" When he replied that he did not, she asked him to lift her veil. The young man did not comply; he was so spooked that he took off running. His friends laughed at him after hearing the story—but then others came forward with their own experiences with the Veiled Lady. One such witness was Charles Jacobs of 51 West Princess Street.

The following Sunday night, Jacobs was walking near the park's fountain when he was approached by a "very tall and thin" woman who asked him to lift her veil. Jacobs, like the others who had been presented with the same strange request, ran away down Beaver Street as fast as he could. At the corner of Princess Street, he met a teenager who was on his way home from church. Jacobs warned the youth to "watch out for the ghost of Penn Park," but the teenager laughed and continued on his journey, but he, too, was approached by the Veiled Lady when he entered the park. He also took off running when she asked him to take a peek under the veil. When he returned home, he told his parents of the strange encounter, and the police were notified.

Despite the police presence, the woman in black continued to make her nightly appearances. Though her identity has never been ascertained, a young man named William Burger was reported to be the only one who dared to accept the woman's challenge and raise the black veil.

According to Burger, he was cutting through the park on his walk home from work on the evening of Monday, October 26, when he encountered the woman near the high school on the grounds of the former potter's field. After she had asked her usual questions, she said: "And do you not recognize me?"

"No," replied Burger.

"Then lift my veil," she said. The young man placed his fingers on the black fabric and lifted it, revealing a young and beautiful face with pearly teeth and dimpled cheeks. Suddenly, she brushed Burger's hand away, and the veil once again concealed her face. By the time Burger was able to regain his composure, the Veiled Lady was gone.

Patrolman Miller, who was the park's night watchman, had heard about the strange woman and told the *Reading Times* that the Veiled Lady had accosted him on three separate occasions. Like William Burger, Patrolman Miller was convinced that she was not a ghost but a living creature of flesh and blood. Though he was unable to detain her, he believed that the apparition was merely a demented woman.

So, who was the mysterious Veiled Lady of Penn Park, and why did she only implore young men to lift her black veil? Was she merely a prankster looking to scare unsuspecting park visitors out of their wits? Or was the park policeman correct in his assumption that she was deranged? If so, one has to wonder what bizarre mental aberration compelled her to dress in funereal clothing and search for a man who recognized her. Had she lost her mind after being deserted by a lover? If such was the case, why did she choose to haunt Penn Park, and why after dark? Did the park hold a special romantic significance in her tortured heart? Maybe she had strolled the park with him on some long ago starry night, holding hands, unaware that this rendezvous might be their last.

These questions are nearly as intriguing as the possibility of a lifelike ghost prowling the grounds of the old potter's field, upset over the desecration of a grave that had been undisturbed since the early 19th century, or perhaps a phantom distraught over the terrible fate of a Union soldier who drew his last breath on the same piece of land where children now play.

19.
BURIED ALIVE: THE HORRIBLE DEATH OF MARY NEWLIN
(CHESTER COUNTY)

On a sunny Sunday in June 1907, a pretty little girl with golden hair walked the short distance home from her grandfather's farm near the village of Avondale. Accompanying five-year-old Mary Robbins Newlin was her little sister, Fannie. At a fork in the road where an old, abandoned church stood, the sisters parted, and it was at this lonesome spot where Mary was last seen alive, clutching a loaf of freshly baked bread her grandparents had given her in one hand and a harmonica—her favorite toy—in the other.

It was believed by District Attorney MacElree, after interviewing members of the Newlin family, that Mary had been either kidnapped or, worse, assaulted and murdered by some fiend lurking in the shadows of the abandoned chapel. On the evening of Wednesday, June 19, the district attorney and his assistant, H.L. Sproat, met with the grandparents and pored over every aspect of the case. John Newlin was a well-to-do farmer, and the Newlin name was respected throughout Chester County; Ellis Newlin, a brother of Mary's grandfather, was the long-time proprietor of the

Madison House in West Chester, and other members of the family were regarded as upstanding pillars of the community. This, of course, caused Sproat and MacElree to ponder the possibility of a kidnapping. But, when no ransom demands were proffered, the district attorney and his assistant began to fear for the worst.

MacElree and Sproat also met with the girl's stepfather, Irwin Lewis, who lived an eighth of a mile from the farm of John Newlin. It was to Lewis' home where Mary had been heading when she disappeared. Lewis immediately called for a search of the countryside, adamant that his stepdaughter had been slain and her body hidden near the scene of her disappearance. The terrain was hilly, and swaths of forest flanked the farmlands, but concerned citizens formed a search party and searched through the night, guided by the lantern of Irwin Lewis. Meanwhile, Constable George Timanus of Avondale led his party of fifteen searchers through the countryside, but no sign of the missing girl could be found.

But there was something strange about Irwin Lewis, though District Attorney MacElree couldn't quite put his finger on it. Was it possible that Lewis knew more about his stepdaughter's fate than he had been letting on? MacElree thought so, and to satisfy his suspicions, he kept a close eye on Lewis, confident that he alone had sufficient motive and opportunity to commit the heinous deed.

At sunrise the following morning, MacElree assembled his team of searchers on the Lewis farm, just as he had done the previous evening. However, when MacElree split his party into two teams and instructed one to search the Lewis property, Irwin protested, arguing that every inch of his farm had been gone over thoroughly the previous day. Reluctantly, he agreed to assist the search party in their efforts, but his reaction only cemented the district attorney's suspicions. MacElree ordered Lewis to accompany the other party, leaving John Shelley and John O'Brien in charge of the party searching the Lewis farm.

Shelley and O'Brien also suspected Irwin Lewis of murdering his stepdaughter, and after Lewis had disappeared with MacElree, they began a focused search on a part of the property where they believed the girl's body had been buried. It was a spot near the barn they had seen the night before, a spot where the soil looked to have been recently disturbed. Shelley and O'Brien began digging, and it did not take them long to uncover the ghastly evidence of Irwin Lewis' crime.

Daylight revealed that Mary Newlin had been strangled with a piece of tarred rope, the kind used by farmers to tie up bundles of wheat. The rope had been doubly knotted and was sunk deep into the flesh of the girl's neck when her body was found. A burlap sack had been placed over the head, and clutched firmly in her hand was a toy harmonica. It must have been this item, the one possession that little Mary prized above all others, that she had held onto desperately like a sacred talisman as the last breaths of life escaped from her tiny body.

Shelley and O'Brien left the barn to relay the news of their gruesome find to Constable Timanus, who, in turn, relayed the message to District Attorney MacElree while Irwin Lewis was out of earshot. MacElree convinced Lewis to follow the men back to the farm. Leading the way to a grove of trees, the district attorney stopped abruptly, wheeled around, and said, "Lewis, the body of the child has been found buried near the barn on your farm." At this announcement, Lewis turned deathly pale and appeared to stagger; the blood drained from his lips, and his skin instantly turned the color of chalk. Shelley and O'Brien thought for a moment that Lewis was going to faint.

"Why did you kill that innocent little girl?" demanded the district attorney.

"No, no!" Lewis protested. "My God! I didn't do it!"

"You murderer!" roared MacElree, who looked as if he were about to strangle Lewis with his bare hands. "You murderer! You dog! Why did you murder that little child?"

In the eerie stillness of the countryside, nothing stirred, and the only sound that could be heard was the gurgling in Lewis' throat as he fumbled for words. "I didn't do it," was all he could manage to blurt out. Constable Timanus led the young man to a waiting buggy, where a small crowd had already assembled. The accused killer spotted his father, Harry Lewis, in the crowd. "Father, help me!" pleaded Irwin. "I never killed little Mary. I always loved her and waited at home, but she did not come. Now they tell me I killed her. I did not! Oh, Lord, save me, save me!"

Mr. Lewis declared that his son was not the killer. "I know Irwin is innocent!" he shouted at the crowd. "The boy didn't do it, nor did I."

The constable transported Lewis a short distance to the scene of the crime, where the girl's mother was sobbing hysterically. "My baby!" she screamed, "Oh, my baby!" She fainted as she heard the buggy approach. A physician was summoned, but as soon as Mrs. Lewis had regained consciousness, she fell into hysterics and fainted again. Someone in the crowd asked Irwin if his father had anything to do with the death of Mary Newlin, but he declared that it must have been a tramp who had murdered his stepdaughter.

John Shelley, a neighboring farmer, later described the discovery of the body. "I own the strip of land beside Lewis' barn, right near where the body was found. Two months ago, Lewis dug two holes for refuse. One of these he had filled up several weeks ago, but the other one was left open until only a few days ago. This aroused my suspicions. When we searched the place on Thursday, we noticed this hole had been filled up with recently turned dirt, and on Friday morning, we set to work to dig it up. Soon after the spades had sunk into the dirt, we turned over something white. It was the corner of the child's dress, and the belt was found next."

Shortly after two o'clock, Deputy Coroner Dickson arrived from Kennett Square and immediately empaneled a jury comprised of neighboring farmers and began the inquest. After viewing the corpse and listening to the statements of the men who had found the body, the jury returned a verdict declaring that Mary Newlin came to her death at the hands of Irwin Lewis.

District Attorney MacElree later said that his most important clue was revealed after he had dug into Mrs. Lewis' past. Five years earlier, Edna Newlin had been employed as a nurse at the Chester County Insane Asylum, where she met and fell in love with an orderly named Lawrence Butler. They were to be married, but Butler skipped town before their wedding day, leaving Edna alone and pregnant. She returned to the home of her father, John Newlin, where the child was born. Irwin and Edna had been childhood sweethearts, and he had known all about Edna's romance with Lawrence Butler, but five months after Butler ditched his bride-to-be, Irwin agreed to marry her and raise the baby girl as his own. However, the presence of little Mary was a constant cause of irritation to Irwin Lewis, or so supposed MacElree, and this was the motive for his callous crime.

Under the cover of darkness, so as not to expose the accused killer to the justice of an angry mob, Constable Timanus delivered Lewis to the Avondale jail, and every effort was made by authorities to keep the fact hidden. The Avondale lock-up was hardly more than a shack adjoining the village firehouse, and it wouldn't have taken much force if vigilantes had planned to storm the facility.

However, a loose-tongued guard let it be known that Irwin Lewis was inside, and this forced MacElree to lie to the press and deny the rumors. Nevertheless, business around town was practically suspended as hundreds flocked to the jail, eager to catch a glimpse of Lewis. Authorities also did their best to keep the time and location of Mary Newlin's funeral a secret. The child's body was taken to a Kennett Square undertaker in an unmarked wagon and hastily buried at the family plot at Union Hill Cemetery.

MacElree also thought it wise not to divulge the details of the coroner's autopsy report—for if this information had leaked out, surely there would be a lynching in Avondale. Physicians who examined the body found that it had been covered from head to toe in bruises, injuries which had been caused by vicious blows from a closed fist. Mary had also been struck on the head with a force sufficient to cause a cerebral hemorrhage. Based on the evidence, MacElree believed that Mary had been sitting by the barn playing her harmonica when she was attacked.

Meanwhile, Irwin Lewis was begging the guard, Tim Maloney, to protect him from the mob that had made its way to the Avondale jail. "My God, don't let them get at me!" pleaded Lewis. It was apparent to Maloney that his prisoner would never be able to hold up under the strain; Lewis reportedly broke into fits of hysterical laughter mingled with tears. When it came time for Lewis to be transported to the county jail at West Chester, the prisoner refused to go outside. "Those men will kill me," he wept. Constable Timanus had to sneak Lewis out the back door while guards created a diversion in front of the jail.

At Kennett Square, the constable ordered Lewis onto a trolley bound for West Chester. As fate would have it, the trolley tracks passed right alongside Union Hill Cemetery, and as the trolley slowly crawled past the freshly filled grave with its little mound of dirt, Lewis grew inconsolable, attempting to shield his face with his manacled hands. Word of his arrival had preceded him, and when the trolley stopped in front of the county jail at the corner of New and Market Streets, Lewis found another angry mob waiting for him. The crowds lingered around the building for hours; it wasn't until late in the evening of Sunday, June 23, that officers finally dispersed them.

MACELREE BUILDS HIS CASE

While the district attorney began plotting his case on behalf of the Commonwealth, Lewis found himself in the hands of two very capable defense attorneys, Thomas Pierce and William Windle. The defense seemed to base its hopes around the possibility that Lewis might be spared from the gallows because of MacElree's over-exuberance. Pierce and Windle, who were related to the accused killer, had attempted to visit their client at Avondale—as they had every legal right to do—but were turned away by Constable Timanus. "You can't see him," the constable had declared. "Those are the instructions I have received."

"By whose authority do you refuse us permission to see Lewis?" demanded Pierce.

"By the authority of the district attorney," Timanus replied.

Pierce and Windle were incensed to discover that MacElree had not only forbidden them access to their client but had immediately left for a vacation in Delaware before the defense counsel had a chance to confront him. Next, they went to the Lewis farm and, with the help of Irwin's father, began to formulate an alibi for their client. This was not an easy task, as Lewis had already told authorities that he had been alone on the farm feeding the chickens at the time of his stepdaughter's murder. But things began to look up for Windle and Pierce when a neighbor farmer, Henry Jacobs, revealed that he had seen two unknown men prowling about the barn on the day of the murder. Lewis' aunt had also seen the same men, but their identity has never been ascertained.

MacElree, of course, could argue that this only suggested that Lewis may not have acted alone, for authorities had already found the loaf of bread that Mary had been carrying in a bag inside the Lewis home, and both Irwin and his wife had told the district attorney previously that Mary had never arrived home after leaving her grandfather's farm. So, how did the bread get there? MacElree hinted to the press that he had many other cards up his sleeve that would ultimately hang Irwin Lewis.

THE FATE OF IRWIN LEWIS

Raving and declaring his innocence, Irwin Lewis became so violent in jail that he was put in a straitjacket by the prison physician, Dr. Scattergood. But this did not prevent his return to Avondale the following morning for the inquest before Justice Lipp. After an impressive presentation of evidence by District Attorney MacElree, Lewis took the witness stand and told a wild story.

"Yes, it is true that I went over to my home at five o'clock on Sunday a week ago. Little Mary Newlin was in the wagon shed when I got there. She fell out of the window, and she was dead when I went to her," explained the young farmer. "I was afraid, and I pulled a bag over her head, then tied a string around her neck and buried her in the hole back of the barn. My God, what will my father think, and what will my mother and my wife think when they hear this?"

But MacElree could not be fooled. Jaws dropped to the floor when the district attorney declared, "This man buried little Mary Newlin while she was yet alive!" He called to the stand Dr. Gifford, who testified that Mary's death had not been caused by her external injuries but that she had succumbed to the torture of being buried alive. At these words, the five hundred men and women in attendance began shouting for Lewis' blood, and Justice Lipp cleared the room before arraigning Lewis and remanding him to prison to await trial.

Although the trial was set to begin in October of 1907, legal wrangling forced the postponement of the case until January of the following year in the defense's futile attempt to have Lewis examined by a lunacy commission. The murder trial concluded on January 31, with the fate of Irwin Lewis resting in the hands of a jury. The insanity defense was a failure, and Lewis was found guilty of murdering five-year-old Mary Newlin. The date of his execution was fixed for February 25, 1909.

Lewis was hanged at 10:07 that morning at the Chester County jail, but not before his uncle made a last-ditch effort to save the killer's life. As the scaffold was being prepared, Curtis Lewis sent a telegram to Governor

Stuart, reading: *Can't you interfere at the last moment on behalf of Irwin A. Lewis? Do so, I beg of you, in the name of humanity.*

No response was received. In all likelihood, the governor had never even read the telegram. In the meantime, Lewis busied himself giving away his worldly possessions; to his father, he bequeathed $800 in savings, and to his brother Wayne he gave a watch and chain. He then walked to the gallows without a quiver of fear and paid for his crime with his life.

Less than an hour before his execution, Irwin Lewis made a final statement:

"If I am guilty of this, I put it all into God's hands to forgive me, for if I did this, I have no recollection of it. I never could have borne up through all these trials if I had had a feeling of guilt. I talked to God last night just as though I were talking to Him in person. I asked Him to give peace and loving kindness to all. I hope little Dorothy will grow up to be a good, useful woman. I feel prepared to meet my Saviour face to face and fully believe I'll meet my dear ones that have gone before up yonder. I die forgiving all my enemies."

Dorothy, a daughter born to Irwin and Edna Lewis on Independence Day of 1904—just two weeks after Mary's death—proved to live up to her father's wishes, passing away peacefully in Massachusetts in 2000 at the age of 92. Edna Newlin Lewis eventually remarried and moved to Massachusetts, where she remained until she died in 1955 at the age of 75. After the execution, Irwin's body was taken to Kennett Square for burial at Union Hill Cemetery, the same graveyard where Mary Newlin had been laid to rest.

20.
THE DISAPPEARING SKELETON
(COLUMBIA COUNTY)

A round noon on Thursday, April 22, 1926, a young man named Royal Phillips ventured into the Brush Valley woods on the grounds of the Roaring Creek Water Company just north of Mount Carmel. He had gone to the woods to assist his brother, Nelson, a state forest inspector, and was walking above the dam towards a safety strip that was being burned at the foot of Patterson Mountain to prevent the spread of forest fires when he stumbled across a human skeleton. After regaining his composure, Royal picked up the skull and raced back to Mount Carmel to report the ghastly find to the chief of police, Abe Morgan. He then took the skull to his home on East Avenue, and so began a mystery that remained unsolved for nearly a century.

The following morning, Charles Madenfort of the Roaring Creek Water Company went to Mount Carmel and, accompanied by Phillips, ventured to the spot where the discovery was made, only to find that the rest of the skeleton was mysteriously missing. Madenfort and Phillips searched the woods for hours but were only successful in locating the tree which Phillips had marked the previous afternoon. The perplexed men then turned the skull over to William Judge of Centralia, the deputy coroner of Columbia

County. Since the water company lands also included Northumberland County, Coroner J.K. Fisher of Sunbury was also notified.

THE SKULL WITH THE GOLDEN TEETH

The authorities discovered a hole in the skull, a little more than an inch in diameter, leading some to suspect foul play. Others, however, believed that animals or the elements could have caused this hole since the skull appeared to have lain in the woods, untouched, for several years. Part of the jaw was missing, along with all but two of the dead man's teeth, which further supported the theory that death must have occurred years earlier. The Mount Carmel *Item* reported that the teeth had been filled with gold. Authorities immediately began to scour the records for missing persons from Brush Valley and the surrounding vicinity, convinced that it would be an easy task to determine who among the missing had their teeth filled with gold. They were sorely mistaken.

THE MYSTERY OF ONE-LEGGED SANDOR

Meanwhile, as word of the discovery spread, locals expressed their opinions as to the identity of the deceased. In nearby Marion Heights, it was whispered that the skeleton belonged to Alexander "Sandor" Kovich, who had been missing from that borough since September 1921. It was recalled that Kovich, a 28-year-old boarder at the home of John Shiko, had an artificial leg, having one of his legs amputated after falling asleep on the highway in a drunken state and nearly freezing to death. Five years had passed without anyone seeing or hearing from Kovich, who was known to have been depressed over his inability to find work after losing his leg. Those who lived in Marion Heights believed that Sandor had been out for a walk near the Roaring Creek dam when he collapsed from exhaustion. Mrs. Shiko, who was certain that Phillips had found the remains of the missing boarder, stated that if the skull were positively identified, she would ask for the skull and give Kovich a proper funeral.

Others believed that the dead man was James Powers, an elderly man who had disappeared from the mining village of Exchange several years earlier. After his disappearance, search parties combed the mountains, exploring every mine breach and crevice between Mount Carmel and

Brush Valley, but their efforts were in vain. As the weekend drew near, the authorities were leaning toward the bones being those of Powers, though they had no tangible evidence to support this theory, and no one seemed to recall whether or not either of these two men had gold fillings.

The possibility of either Kovich or Powers having gold fillings seems highly unlikely, as both men were impoverished coal miners, and the disappearance of the skeleton just hours after its discovery by Royal Phillips only adds to the mystery. Were the remains of an unknown murder victim hastily removed from the scene after word of its discovery reached Mount Carmel? Or had Phillips and Madenfort simply been mistaken about where the find had been made? Ultimately, the case was never cracked, and the missing bones have never been accounted for.

21.

THE GHOST TRAIN OF CARROLLTOWN

(CAMBRIA COUNTY)

Were it not for the famous Lizzie Borden murder trial taking place five hundred miles away in Fall River, Massachusetts, the bizarre story of the phantom train of Carrolltown might have become well-known outside of Cambria County. The tiny borough of Carrolltown sits about twenty miles west of Altoona and, in 1892, became a stop on the newly-formed Cambria & Clearfield Railroad, which was part of the Susquehanna Branch (Altoona Division) of the Pennsylvania Railroad. The focal point of this rail line was a tunnel constructed through Strittmatter Hill, just south of Carrolltown, and it was near this spot where one of the strangest events in Pennsylvania history took place.

In August of 1892, the nation's attention turned to a courthouse in New England, where witnesses took the stand in what would become one of America's most famous murder trials. Meanwhile, in Cambria County, the citizens of Carrolltown were excited over the coming of the railroad, hopeful that it would bring a new level of prosperity to the sleepy little village. Over the previous year, many of the locals eagerly watched the construction crews working along Plank Road, where scores of laborers, most of whom were Italian immigrants, hustled to complete their tasks.

However, not everyone was preoccupied with the coming of the railroad. One night in early August, two men named Suef (or Sueffert, in other accounts), along with their wives, were driving their wagons along Plank Road over Strittmatter Hill at around eleven o'clock when their horses suddenly grew agitated and excited. The Suefs, who were from out of town and hampered by the darkness, had no idea they were standing atop a railroad tunnel. But then, a shrill blast from a steam whistle pierced the night. Since the sound seemed to be coming from beneath their feet, it soon became clear they were standing on top of the new 900-foot tunnel that all of Carrollstown had been talking about. There was just one tiny little problem—the opening of the Cambria & Clearfield Railroad was still several days away. In fact, the tunnel project had not yet been completed. Strange, they thought, but the shrill cry of the whistle was just the beginning of the strangeness of that night.

A HARBINGER OF DEATH

Just seconds after hearing the mysterious whistle, the Suef family observed a puff of smoke, mingled with flame, from a passenger train that emerged from the tunnel. The Suefs, being practical people, immediately concluded that the new railroad had opened early to travel, and they watched as the passenger train chugged rapidly northward. Moments later, they heard the loudest and ghastliest noise they had ever encountered—an otherworldly screaming, like the tormented cries of victims of some unimaginable tragedy, which left them covering their ears and trembling in terror. Just when they recovered their senses, things got worse; following the ear-piercing wail came the sound of a tremendous crash. The Suefs watched in horror as a carriage carrying a man and a woman was tossed high into the air in the distance as the train rounded the Eckenrode Mills curve and disappeared into nothingness.

Others heard the train but did not see it. In a story about the bizarre event appearing in the Pittsburgh *Daily Post* on August 31, 1892, it is stated: *Residents of that vicinity, among them being Mr. Tinesmith, say that each night about 11 o'clock, the phantom train may be heard, but nothing is visible. Those who witnessed this strange affair are firm in the belief that this demonstration was but a premonition of a catastrophe that will occur on the road.*

Of course, the problem with tales of premonitions and omens is that we often hear about them after the tragedy has already taken place. Many of us recall hearing after-the-fact claims of premonitions following 9/11 and the space shuttle *Challenger* disaster, for instance. Most of the time, this causes us to raise a skeptical brow and say, "Well, that information would have been useful *before* the catastrophe." In this manner, we can weed out dubious claims. What makes the Carrolltown incident unique, however, is that newspaper stories about the impending crash—which occurred in September of that year—began circulating days before the first train passed over the Cambria & Clearfield tracks. At least four persons saw the phantom train, while dozens more heard the ghostly whistles and wails.

CURSED FROM THE BEGINNING

At 12:01 on the morning of August 22, 1892, the Cambria & Clearfield Railroad was formally opened to passenger and freight traffic by Superintendent W.N. Bannard. Appointed to the position of trainmaster was W.C. Snyder, and filling the positions of freight conductors were Rutter and Brown, while the passenger conductors were McDermitt and Rush. This new rail line, totaling seventy miles, would bring to market the coal from the fields of Punxsutawney and the lumber from the vast timber tracts of Clearfield County. The sleepy village of Carrolltown was sure to experience an economic boom, it was believed, and plans were made to build a passenger station in town.

The Cambria & Clearfield was comprised of several branches: The Cush Creek branch, the Hastings branch, the Ebensburg branch, and the Susquehanna branch, the latter of which passed through Carrolltown and was the home of the Strittmatter Tunnel. While the other branches were opened on August 22, the Susquehanna branch would not be opened until September, when the tunnel would be finished and the passenger station complete. The reason for the delay was because of the complexity of building the 900-foot-long tunnel. Under the supervision of Superintendent J.D. Lasher, the project pushed forward rapidly, but Lasher, who was known to be a heavy drinker, was either fired or resigned from his position, necessitating the finding of his replacement, thereby causing delays to the tunnel project. On September 19, 1891, Lasher died at the Blair

County poorhouse, where he had been brought five days earlier after a drinking binge. It was reported that Lasher had lost $10,000 in a failed tunnel project in the South shortly before his death. Construction of the tunnel progressed rapidly under Lasher's successor, resulting in several fatal accidents to workers. In February of 1892, several immigrant workers were injured, one fatally, by an accidental dynamite explosion. This was the second fatal construction accident in as many weeks.

THE WRECK AT LINK'S CUT

Shortly after six o'clock on the evening of Thursday, September 8, 1892, a train carrying one hundred railroad workers, most of them Italian immigrants, was traveling to a point on the recently-completed Susquehanna branch of Cambria & Clearfield Railroad to a spot where repairs were needed. At the curve at the Link farm near Eckenrode Mills—the spot where the phantom passenger train had disappeared a month earlier—the southbound work train, consisting of engine, tender and three cars, collided headfirst with a northbound passenger train, which, only moments before, had emerged from the Strittmatter Tunnel.

Wreckage filled the deep, narrow cut near Eckenrode Mills, and survivors immediately began searching the steaming hot mass of tangled metal for fellow passengers and workmen. Nine bodies were pulled from the wreckage, including those of engineer C.W. Ferry and fireman Raymond Parrish of the passenger train, timekeeper W.S. Rowland, Edward Ahles, Samuel Rich, Alex Godolly, and Italian laborers Guiseppe Martino, Martin Martino and Anton DiNelle. Joseph Cochios and Tony Franco were transported to a hospital in Altoona for severe steam burns. The death toll would continue to rise over the next several hours as additional victims, all of them Italians, succumbed to their injuries.

It was soon discovered that the cause of the crash had been insubordination; G.S. Yoder, the engineer of the work train, had disobeyed orders after he was told to lay over on the side track at Patton to allow the passenger train to pass. A search was made for Yoder and the conductor of the work train, G.E. Dunne, both of whom had apparently decided to run away from the scene to avoid the wrath of the survivors. A few days later, Yoder and Dunne emerged from hiding and were both present at the coroner's inquest. According to witness statements, the two trains didn't see each other until the moment before impact due to the Link's Cut curve. The engineer and foreman of the work train saved themselves by jumping from the cab. The others weren't so lucky; of the fourteen who would eventually die from the crash, seven were roasted alive by escaping steam and killed instantly.

On Tuesday, September 13, a jury empaneled by Coroner McGough concluded that "C.W. Ferry and others came to their death by the collision of a construction train and a passenger train on the Cambria & Clearfield Railroad, in Carroll Township, Cambria County, on the 8th day of September, and that said collision was caused by the gross negligence and disobedience of rules and regulations covering the operation of the said railroad, by G.E. Dunne, conductor of the construction train, and G.S. Yoder, engineer of the construction train."

Today, the Strittmatter Tunnel is abandoned, and the footprint of the tracks left by the old Cambria & Clearfield Railroad is paved over or reclaimed by nature. Shortly after the crash at Link's Cut, the railroad was shaken up by a change in management after its detachment from the Altoona Division, with H.D. Lovell taking over as superintendent. In 1905, in order to improve safety, the Pennsylvania Railroad decided to reroute its passenger tracks around the tunnel and the dangerous curve near the Link farm. The PRR continued to use the tunnel for coal trains until 1960, when a cave-in injured three railroad workers. Because of the September 1892 crash, Carrolltown never became a thriving hub of business and commerce; when the passenger station was robbed in December of 1893, the Altoona *Tribune* reported that the bandits made off with the princely sum of thirty-eight cents.

22.

THE POISONER OF GRAY'S ALLEY

(ALLEGHENY COUNTY)

One of America's most successful serial killers was Martha Grinder, an Allegheny County woman who rose to notoriety in the years following the Civil War as "The Poisoner of Gray's Alley." What made Martha Grinder so successful in playing her deadly game, aside from the fact that she killed indiscriminately for years before getting caught, was that she appeared beyond reproach—for Martha was adored by her neighbors and was regarded as one of the most kind-hearted women in the Pittsburgh area. If Mrs. Grinder had perpetrated her sinister crimes in the modern era, there's no doubt that her name would be known far and wide. But since she carried out her mission of misery in the early days of mass communication (the telegraph had been invented when Martha was still a teenager), her name is now just a footnote in the annals of Pennsylvania crime.

Prior to 1907, Pittsburgh's North Side was a separate municipality known as Allegheny City. During the closing years of the Civil War, hospitals and nurses were few and far between in the city. For residents of Old Allegheny, middle-aged Martha Grinder was an angel of mercy in the community; wherever there was sickness, Mrs. Grinder was summoned as one might summon St. Anthony to assist in locating a missing object.

Martha spent many nights keeping bedside vigils for sick neighbors, and she cooked meals for the husbands of sick wives. She was rarely seen without her "miraculous" beef broth and herbal tea, which she readily dispensed to anyone gripped by fever. Martha was a tiny woman but carried herself with an air of graceful dignity, which her patients found comforting. The ill seemed to have a fascination for Martha, and the fascination was mutual; she had a habit of intently studying the faces of her patients, watching each symptom as it developed. Once invited inside a patient's home, Martha took complete charge, bearing the burden of a nurse, caretaker, and cook. There was never a nurse as thorough as Mrs. Grinder, said her neighbors. If one of her patients should die, she dressed the body for burial and made the necessary funeral arrangements. As a result, Martha was praised for her commitment to her patients and was seen as the personification of self-sacrifice.

Yet, no one knew much about her past. She had arrived in Allegheny City around 1860 with her second husband, George Grinder. They were poor and rented a cheap house near the Point. They brought with them a baby girl, who was about one year old. After about a year the Grinders moved to a better house in Gray's Alley, and it was around this time Martha began wearing finer clothes and carrying herself as a pillar of the community. She joined the Methodist Episcopal Church but soon resigned after a quarrel with some of the congregation. When questioned about her sudden affluence, Martha explained that a relative had left her $10,000 in a will that stipulated that Martha would only receive the bequest if she brought forth a child to carry on the family bloodline. Rather than scaling back her workload, the sudden windfall made Martha work even harder at caring for the ill. In the summer of 1865, Martha Grinder took on her last patient. Little did she know at the time that this patient would ultimately lead her to the gallows.

Mary Caroline Carothers was the 25-year-old wife of James A. Carothers, and the young couple lived in Gray's Alley next door to the Grinders. One day in June, Martha invited Mary over for tea and peaches and cream. The two women must've presented a stark contrast; Mrs. Carothers was young, beautiful and radiated good health, while Mrs. Grinder was worn down, her hair sprinkled with gray, her body growing thin and frail. Yet, later that evening, it was Mary Carothers who appeared to be at death's door, having fallen ill shortly after tea with Martha Grinder.

Martha jumped into action, as she always did at the first signs of sickness. She made soup and toast for the sick woman and sat at her bedside, wearing an expression of deep compassion. Mary soon began to feel better but fell ill once more after eating one of Martha's meals. A physician, Dr. Irish, was sent for, and he examined Mary. After Martha had left the room, Dr. Irish told the patient's husband that something was seriously wrong, but he kept his opinions as to the true nature of Mary's illness to himself; he did not dare to make accusations that he could not prove. Instead, he urged James Carothers to take Mary out of the area for a while, insisting that a change of scenery would do her good. James complied, and he took his wife to New Castle, where James remained until July 7.

Upon returning to Allegheny City, James learned that Martha Grinder's baby girl had passed away, and James paid a visit to the Grinder home to express his sympathy. However, he noted that Martha wasn't quite as emotional as she should have been over the death of an only child. Martha asked James to stay for breakfast, and she put on a pot of coffee. James later recalled that the coffee had a strange metallic taste, though it did not occur to him to say anything at the time. Martha told James that he looked pale, and her eyes brightened when James confessed that he was feeling a little under the weather. "If you're sick during the night, let me know," said Martha as James took his leave. The young man thought it was a rather strange remark but, once again, did not say anything. Sure enough, James Carothers became violently ill that evening, and Mrs. Grinder was summoned. She brought toast and coffee to the sick man, and James' condition only grew worse after eating.

On July 14, Mary Carothers returned home from New Castle to find her husband ill. She had intended to cook rice and milk that evening, but when she realized that she was out of milk, she went next door to borrow some from Mrs. Grinder. James ate the rice and milk, and his condition took a turn for the worse. Over the next few days, Mary was so busy caring for her husband that she didn't have the time to cook her own meals. As usual, Martha Grinder was quick to volunteer. After eating one of Mrs. Gringer's meals, Mary grew ill and never got out of bed again; she died on August 1, with her husband lying in the same room.

A post-mortem examination revealed a lethal quantity of arsenic and antimony in Mary Carothers' stomach. On August 24, James appeared before a magistrate and filed a complaint against Martha Grinder, accusing her of the murder of his wife. Only then did neighbors connect the dots. They noticed that sickness and Mrs. Grinder were an inseparable pair. Their mistake had simply been that Martha did not follow sickness, but that sickness followed Martha. It was soon recalled that George Grinder's brother, Samuel, had also died while under Martha's care. And then there was Martha's young daughter. And what had happened to Martha's first husband? A chilling picture began to emerge, especially after recalling the tragic fate of eighteen-year-old Jane Buchanan.

On February 24, 1864, the Grinders hired a young Irish woman, Jane Buchanan, as a domestic servant. It was strange, some thought, that a couple of such ordinary means should hire someone to do the cooking and cleaning in a house that was hardly more than a hovel. Jane fell ill soon after her arrival, and one neighbor later recalled that she had detected a strange gleam of delight in Martha's eyes when she refused to offer the sick girl a glass of water. Jane died in agony on February 28, just four days after her arrival. At the time of her death, Jane was engaged to be married.

TRIAL AND EXECUTION

Martha Grinder was formally charged with murder and found guilty on October 28, 1865. During the trial, a tearful James Carothers related the story of his wife's illness, while Martha impassively listened to the testimony without exhibiting the slightest hint of emotion. The courtroom was packed that day, and the spectators anxiously listened to the expert testimonies of Professor Gillson of the Western University of Pennsylvania (now the University of Pittsburgh) and celebrated chemist Otto Wuth. But the crucial moment came when a servant girl testified that Mrs. Grinder had sent her to purchase antimony. Several other witnesses testified that they, too, had fallen ill after dining or drinking tea with Martha Grinder. These included Mrs. Phillips (Mary Carothers' mother), Nancy McCune, Mrs. Ashbaugh, Charlotte Grinder (George and Samuel's sister), Mrs. McBride, Mrs. Morningstar, Mrs. Reynolds, and Margaret Smith and her three children. Pittsburgh newspaper reporter William J. Lytle remarked, in 1930, that "the record of the trial reads like an account of an epidemic." Judge James P. Sterrett sentenced her on November 25 and she was to be hanged the following January. But there was still hope for Martha; Governor Curtin was opposed to capital punishment, and it was whispered that he might give her a reprieve. He did not. When Sheriff John H. Stewart entered her cell and read the death warrant, Martha screamed hysterically at the realization of her fate.

On two occasions, Martha attempted to poison herself while in jail awaiting her execution. The first time, her life was saved by a prison physician. The second time, she did not actually take the poison—it had been discovered inside her cell before she had an opportunity to cheat the hangman. An unidentified individual (who some believe to have been Mrs. Grinder's attorney) had evidently smuggled the poison into the jail. The bottle was found behind a picture frame in her cell, along with a note that read: *We have done all for you that we can. This is a last resort.* The note was signed, "A Friend."

Martha recovered her composure the night before her execution, meticulously arranging her hair to make herself presentable for her dance with death. On January 19, 1866, Martha walked to the scaffold, where she declared, "I am a great, great sinner, but Christ is a great, great Savior." She remained calm as her arms were pinioned. "I am going to heaven, and I hope to meet you there," she said to the sheriff before he placed the rope around her neck. After her face was covered with a white hood, the trap was sprung at one o'clock, and Martha dropped, though, on her descent, the rope slipped a little, and death was caused by strangulation. After thirty minutes, Martha's body was cut down, and she was buried at Hilldale Cemetery (also known as Union Dale Cemetery) later that night under the cover of darkness.

Before her execution, Martha signed a confession acknowledging guilt in the cases of Mary Carothers and Jane Buchanan but denied killing her daughter. However, it was believed that twelve persons may have been fatally—and intentionally- poisoned by Martha Grinder. There is evidence to support this claim, as the body of Samuel Grinder was exhumed and its stomach contents analyzed. Sure enough, a lethal amount of arsenic was discovered. *That her poisoning operations have been carried on for many years, we have no doubt,* reported the Pittsburgh *Post-Gazette* on September 16, 1865. *Perhaps no complete record of their extent and fatality will ever be written except upon the book of the Recording Angel.*

While no complete record of Martha Grinder's crimes was ever written, that didn't stop opportunistic publishers from attempting to cash in on the sensational story. On January 23, 1866—just four days after Martha's execution—publisher John P. Hunt & Co. ran newspaper advertisements hawking a new book entitled *The Life and Confessions of Martha Grinder, The Poisoner.*

ABOUT THE AUTHOR

MARLIN BRESSI is the author of several nonfiction books, including *Hairy Men in Caves: True Stories of America's Most Colorful Hermits* and the *Pennsylvania Oddities* series, which is based on his blog and podcast of the same name. As a writer, his fiction has appeared in *Suspense Magazine*, *Black Cat Mystery Magazine*, *Sherlock Holmes Mystery Magazine*, and other publications.

www.ingramcontent.com/pod-product-compliance
Lightning Source LLC
Chambersburg PA
CBHW030939090426
42737CB00007B/475